·MAT·

Produced and designed by **Matteo Sola**
e.mat@mat-design.com
   www.mat-design.com

happybooKs

Published and distributed by **Happy Books** s.r.l.
P.O. BOX 541 CPO - MO • ITALY
t.0039.059.454219
f.0039.059.450343
e.happy@happybooks.it
   www.happybooks.it

 reno grafica

Pre-press and printing by **renografica** s.r.l.
Bologna - Italy

CLUB FLYER BIZNESS

THE STORY OF THE HUMBLE CLUB FLYER IS ONE OF AN EVOLUTION.
AN EVOLUTION, WHICH DIRECTLY MIRRORS THE RISE OF DANCE MUSIC AND CLUB, CULTURE OVER THE LAST
25 YEARS. WHAT WAS ONCE ONLY A BASIC MEANS OF COMMUNICATING INFORMATION SUCH AS, THIS PLACE,
THIS TIME, THIS MUCH, HAS BECOME A DIVERSE MEDIUM ALLOWING ANY AND ALL FORMS OF VISUAL EXPRESSION
TO BE UTILISED. TO GRAB THE ATTENTION OF THE POTENTIAL CLUBBER AND HELP THEM TO DECIDE THAT THIS
EVENT OR NIGHT IS WORTH GOING TO.

BACK IN THE DAYS THE SCENE WAS SMALL.
IN LONDON IN THE MID 80s ALL YOU NEEDED TO DO WAS GO INTO SOHO, TRADITIONALLY THE HEART OF THE
CITY'S CLUB SCENE AND IN PARTICULAR A PUB CALLED THE "SPICE OF LIFE". ON ANY GIVEN WEEKEND A SMALL
GROUP OF LIKE MINDED INDIVIDUALS WOULD GATHER TO SOCIALISE AND FLYERS WOULD BE PASSED OUT. THEY
WERE BASIC CUT AND PASTE, HAND DRAWN PIECES OF PHOTO COPIED PAPER BUT THEY GAVE YOU THE INFO
THAT YOU NEEDED: WHERE AND WHEN, AS WELL AS WHO MAY BE DJING, (ALTHOUGH THE DJ WAS NOT AT THE
TIME AS POWERFUL A DRAW AS HE OR SHE MAYBE TODAY).

SOME OF THESE EARLIER FLYERS WERE BEAUTIFUL IN THEIR SIMPLICITY AND WERE QUITE DIFFERENT FROM
WHAT HAS BECOME POSSIBLE NOWADAYS WITH THE ALMOST UNIVERSAL ACCESS TO COMPUTERS AND GRAPHIC
PACKAGES.

AS THE DANCE SCENE AND IN PARTICULAR THE WAREHOUSE SCENE BEGAN TO KICK OFF THERE WAS A WHOLE
GENERATION WHO BEGAN TO REALISE THAT YOU DIDN'T NEED A TRADITIONAL CLUB SPACE TO THROW A PARTY.
FIND AN ABANDONED SPACE, BRING THE SOUND, THE DRINK AND THE PEOPLE AND THAT'S ALL YOU NEEDED.
THE FLYER WAS THE INFORMER. IN A FEW SHORT YEARS THE SCENE HAD BECOME SO SUCCESSFUL THAT THE
SPIRIT OF COMPETITION INEVITABLY STARTED TO REAR ITS HEAD. IT WAS IN THIS ENVIRONMENT THAT THE FLYER
AS WE KNOW IT TODAY WAS BORN. WITH SO MANY PARTIES STARTING TO HAPPEN AS WELL AS CLUBS WANTING
A PIECE OF THE ACTION THAT THEY WERE MISSING, THE CHALLENGE WAS ON, TO CAPTURE THE IMAGINATION
OF THE PEOPLE.

A REVOLUTION IN GRAPHICS WAS BEGINNING WITH PEOPLE SUCH AS SWIFTY OR TREVOR JACKSON IN LONDON
SHAPING AND FORMING THE IDENTITY FOR VARIOUS MUSIC SCENES SUCH AS THE ACID JAZZ OR HIP-HOP
MOVEMENTS THAT WERE BUILDING MOMENTUM. THESE STORIES WERE BEING MIRRORED ACROSS THE WORLD
AS CLUB CULTURE UNDERWENT AN UNPRECEDENTED EXPLOSION IN POPULARITY.

THE PAGES OF THIS BOOK CONTAIN A SMALL INSIGHT INTO THE CREATIVITY THAT HAS BEEN EMPLOYED TO
PRODUCE MEMORABLE IMAGES IN THE FORM OF THE CLUB FLYER. IT WOULD TAKE MANY MORE VOLUMES THAN
THIS ONE TO FULLY EXPLORE THIS SUBJECT BUT YOU HAVE TO START SOMEWHERE AND I THINK THAT THIS
COLLECTION OF FLYERS IS A GOOD TO BEGIN A PLACE AS ANY. HERE'S TO THE PAST AND ON TO THE FUTURE.

FRASER COOKE
LONDON 11.12.2002

CLUB FLYER BIZNESS

どこにでもあるクラブフライヤーの歴史は１つの進展です。

フライヤーは過去２５年以上にわたってダンスミュージックやクラブそしてカルチャーに比例して発展してきました。

それは場所、時間などの情報を伝えるというごくシンプルな手段であり、

クラバー達にこのイベント、ナイトは行く価値ありと決めさせる様々なビジュアル表現を利用した、それまでとは異なった表現手段となりました。

しかしひと昔は今とは違い小さな事だったのです。

８０年代半ばのロンドンでは中心街ソーホーに軒を並べるクラブ、特にSpice of Lifeというパブに行く事が全てで、毎週末になると小さなサークルが人を集め、そしてそれと共にフライヤーも人々の手に渡っていきました。

それらは手描きのコピー用紙が切り貼りされたごくベーシックな物でしたが、いつ、どこで、誰がDJをするのかなど、必要な情報を伝えるという役割は果たしていました。(その頃、DJは今の様に魅力のあるものではありませんでしたが)

初期フライヤーの中には、今日可能になったのコンピューターおよびグラフィックパッケージを利用した一般的なそれとはかなり違ったシンプルで美しい物がありました。

ダンスシーン、特にウエアハウスシーンが始まりかけの頃、パーティーを開くのにトライディショナルなクラブスペースは必要ないと悟る世代が出てきました。

必要なのは、放棄されたスペースを探し、音を持ち込み、それからドリンク、後は人を集めるだけでした。

そしてフライヤーが情報源となっていたのです。

何年もしない内にこのシーンは大成功を遂げ、必然的に競争も始まりました。

これが、私たちの知っている今日のフライヤーが生まれた環境だったのです。

多くのパーティーが開かれ始めるにつれ、クラブではそれまでの活気が無くなっていきました、人々の想像力を捕らえるための挑戦が始まったのです。

グラフィック革命はロンドンのSwiftyまたはTrevor Jacksonなどにより始められました。彼等はこの推進力のもとになったAcid JazzやHip-Hopムーブメントなど様々なミュージックシーンの独自性を表現したりしました。

これらの事は世界中に反映し,クラブカルチャー人気は前例のない爆発的増加をたどっていったのです。

この本にはフライヤーという形で歴史に残るべきイメージを生むのにに用いられた創造性に対する洞察が軽く含まれています。

このテーマを完全に探求するにはこの本よりもっと多くの物が必要でしょう、しかしその出発点としてこのフライヤーコレクションは良いものだと思います。過去へそして未来へ向けて。

SEISHO SUMIDA
JAPANESE TRANSLATION

JUNK

ARTWORKS BY: SWIFTY, ANDREW ARNOLD,
MAT, TYLER ASKEW, VÂR, FORMO3

designed by: **Swifty**

EVERY THURSDAY BASS CLEF CORONET ST LONDON N1

TAX £4.50

(8PM) TILL LATE

"*patrick forge's* !!!

!!!!!!!!!!!!!!!!!!!!!!!!
!!!!!!!!!!!!!!!!!!!!!!!!
!!!!!!!!!!!!!!!!!!!!!!!!
!!!!!!!!!!!!!!!!!!!!!!!!
!!!!!!!!!!!!!!!!!!!!!!!!
!!!!!!!!!!!!!!!!!!!!!!!!

!!! *a different bag*"

designed by: **Swifty**

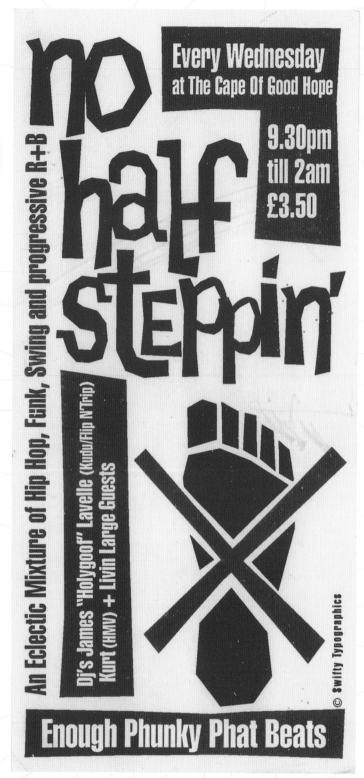

designed by: **Swifty**

AN OFFICIAL THANG THROWN BY — SPEECH AND TAREE OF ARRESTED DEVELOPMENT

DA BiG JUKE JOiNt OF 1993

THURSDAY JANUARY 14TH 1993 FROM **10PM** TILL **6AM** IN DA MORNING
AT THE **INTERNATIONAL BALLROOM**, 620 BUFORD HWY. ATLANTA GA
TICKETS: **ADV (TICKET MASTER)** AND **B4 MIDNIGHT** ON DOOR ARE **TEN BILLS** (12 BILLS AFTER 12AM)

NUTS, FRUITS AND BERRIES FROM THE GARDEN OF EATIN, POETRY READING, AFRICAN VENDORS
ON THE WHEELS OF STEEL, FROM N.Y. KOOL **DJ RED ALERT**

BRING A CAN FOOD
ITEM FOR THE
HOMELESS (UPRISING)

FOR MORE NOIZE AND INFO CONTACT CONSCIOUS COUNTRY COMMITTEE (C.C.C) P.O. BOX 91232 ATL. GA. 30364 (404) 209-7822   100% RECYCLED BOARD. © SWIFTY TYPOGRAFIX

designed by: **Swifty**

THURSDAYS AT THE COMEDY CAFE RIVINGTON ST EC2 £5 £3 CONC £2 WITH FLYER

DJ'S DAVE HUCKER /COLM CARTY

GRIS

8.30PM TILL LATE

A GLOBAL SHIMMY N' SHAKE

GRIS

designed by: **Swifty**

designed by: **Swifty**

shake and fingerpop productions present

friday 17th april 10pm-5am · dj's norman jay/bro marco/femi

shake & fingerpop

92
+ good times

"the long good friday" at villa stephano next to holborn tube

£10

designed by: **Swifty**

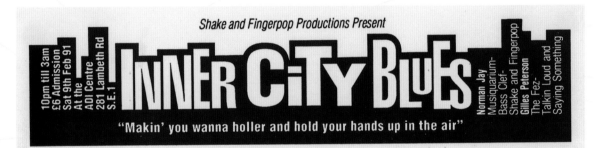

designed by: **Swifty**

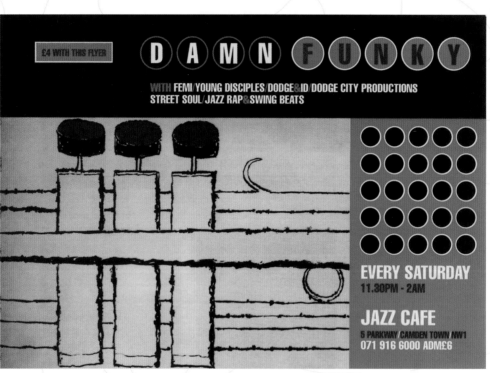

author unknown

© SWIFTY TYPOGRAFIX

JAZZ POWER

GREEN & YELLOW OR GREE

BROWN OR

N BLUE OR BLACK

CORD GR

£5
Thursday 22nd Sept

@ NO 9 / 9 YOUNG STREET, LONDON W8 (OFF KENSINGTON HIGH ST, NEXT TO BARKER'S STORE)

DJ'S: GILLES PETERSON PATRICK FORGE 10.00pm till 3.00am

TO CELEBRATE THE LAUNCH OF BRAZILICA!,- TALKIN' JAZZ 2 & U.F.O. (NO SOUND IS TOO TABOO)

designed by: **Swifty**

designed by: **Swifty**

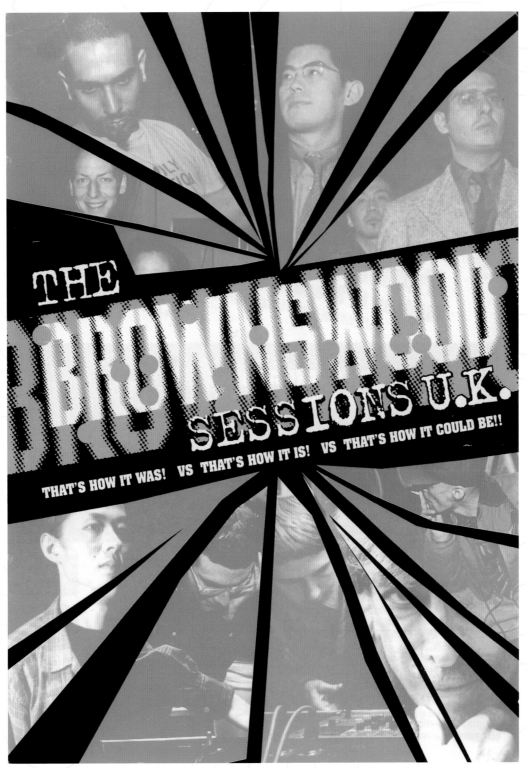

THE BROWNSWOOD SESSIONS U.K.

THAT'S HOW IT WAS! VS THAT'S HOW IT IS! VS THAT'S HOW IT COULD BE!!

designed by: **Swifty**

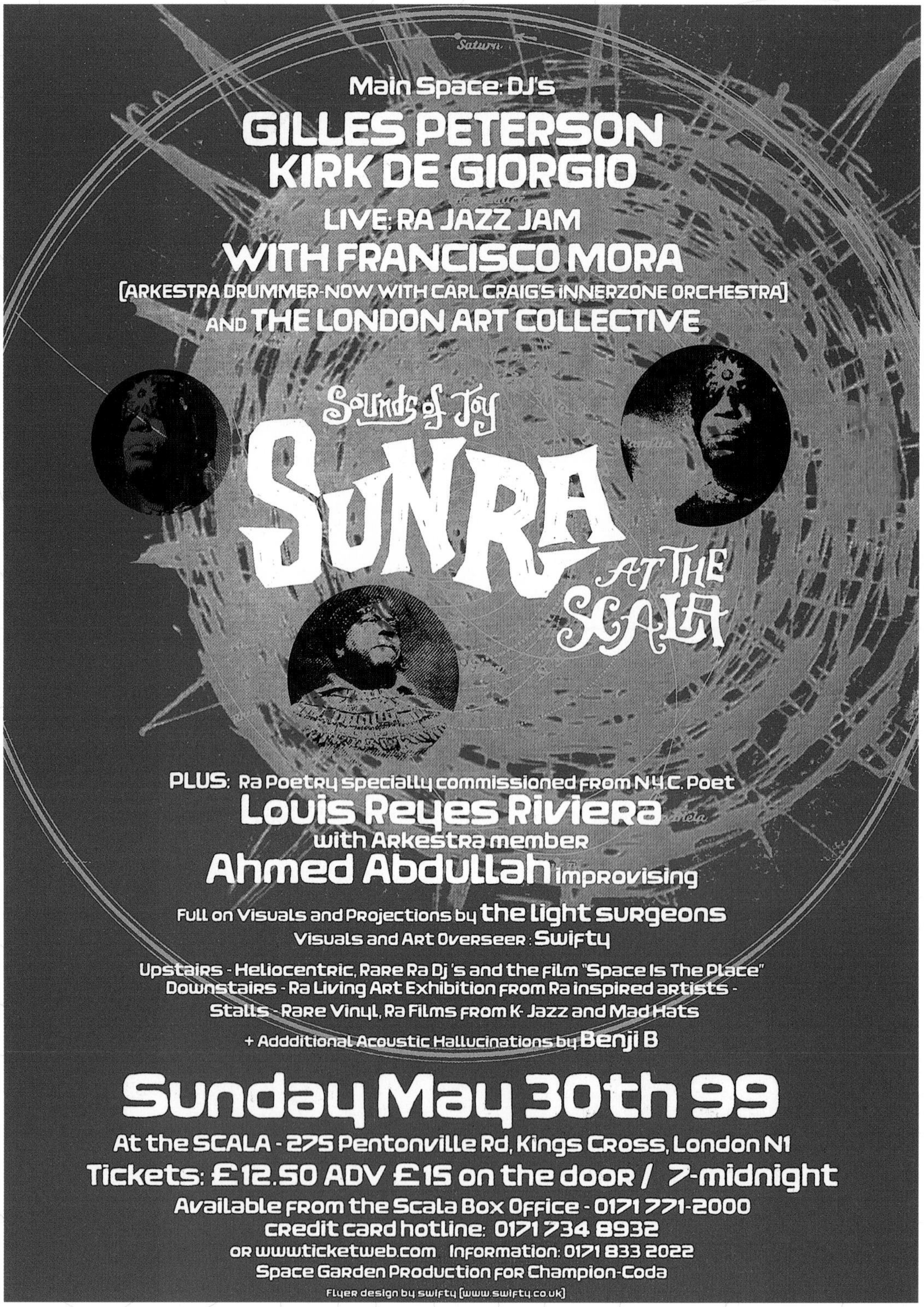

designed by: **Swifty**

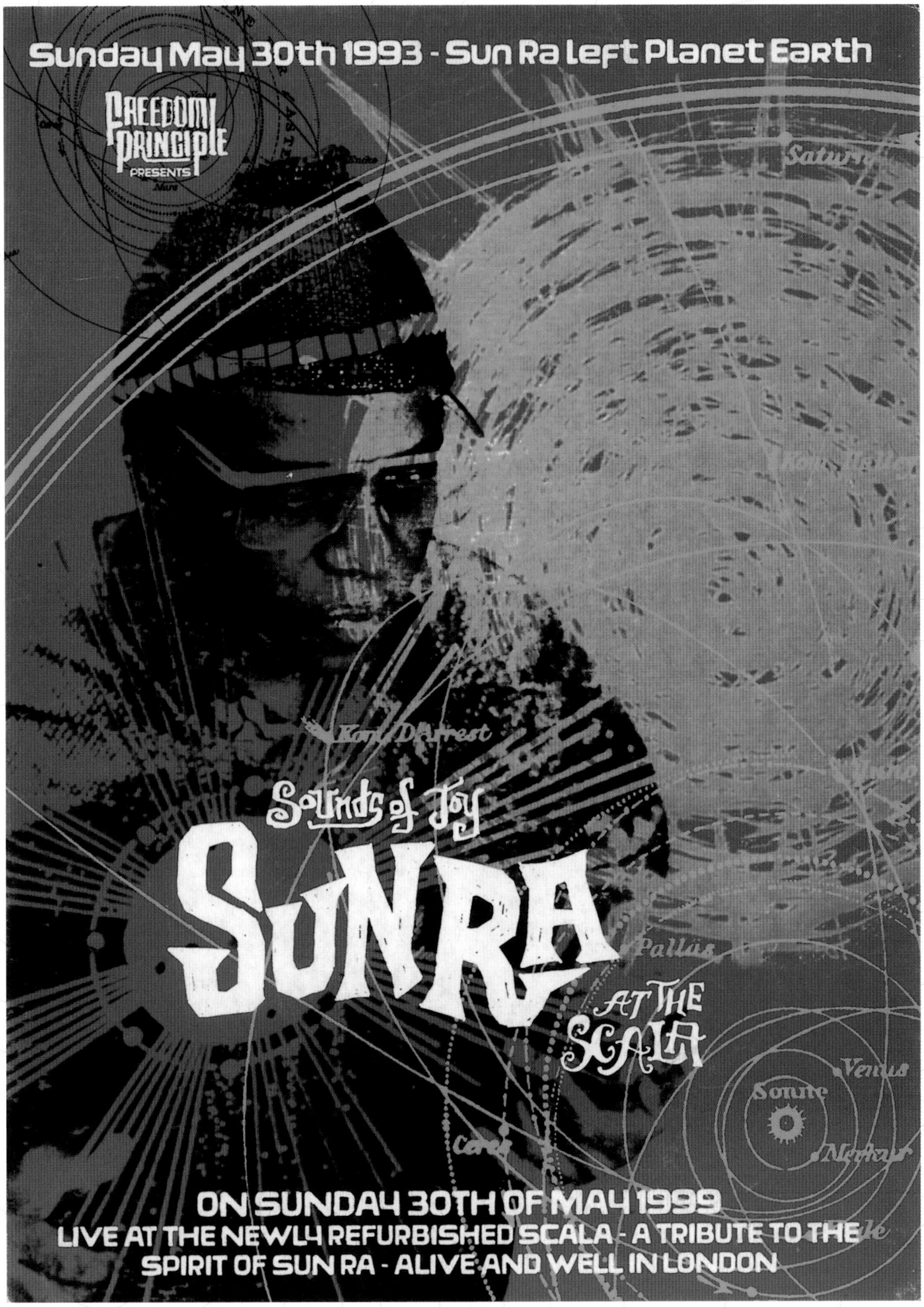

Sunday May 30th 1993 - Sun Ra Left Planet Earth

Sounds of Joy
SUN RA
AT THE SCALA

ON SUNDAY 30TH OF MAY 1999
LIVE AT THE NEWLY REFURBISHED SCALA - A TRIBUTE TO THE
SPIRIT OF SUN RA - ALIVE AND WELL IN LONDON

designed by: Swifty

designed by: **Andrew Arnold**

trans.audio sessions
tyler askew / straight no chaser
local 12 / dj set

thursday
september 19
music @ 11 pm

candela bar
calle san sebastian
no. 110

poster by tylernskew.com

designed by: **Tyler Askew**

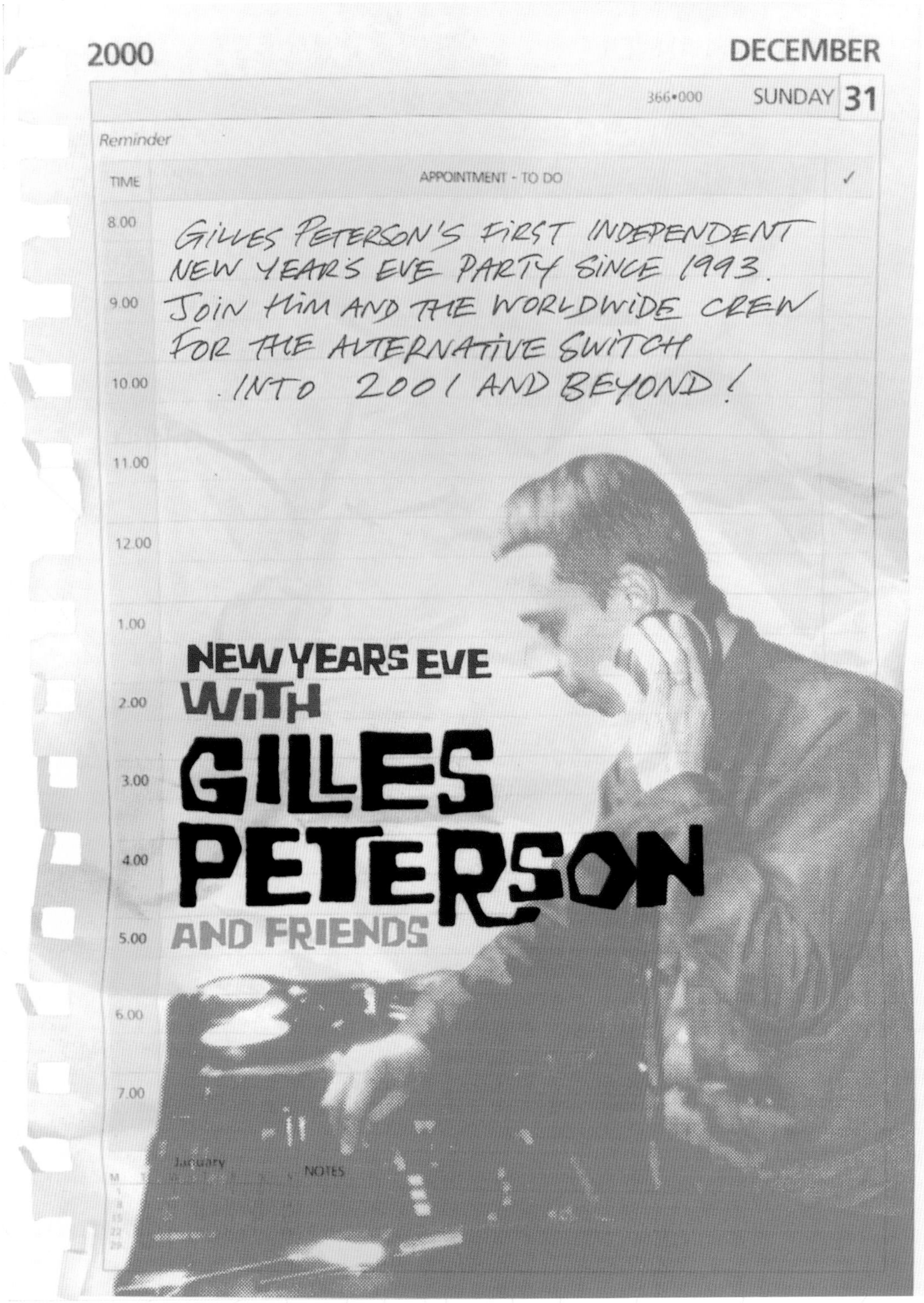

designed by: **Swifty**

designed by: **Vår**

clubmetro

23. juni :: **future sound of jazz**
fauna flash_compost rec. muenchen
rainer trueby_compost rec. rootdown | freiburg
jazzanova_compost rec. berlin

METRO friedrichshafen* ++49 (0) 75 41.37 16 61 * www.club-metro.de

designed by: **Form03**

BRASILEIRA

ARTWORKS BY: SWIFTY
A MUSIC LOVER !

designed by: **Swifty**

BRAZILIAN EXPLOSION !
BATMACUMBA

designed by: **Swifty**

designed by: **Swifty**

designed by: **Swifty**

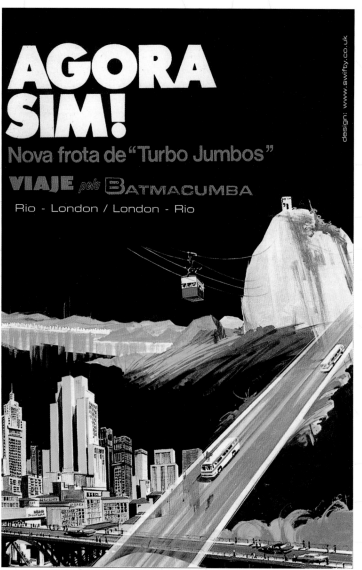

designed by: **Swifty**

designed by: **Swifty**

designed by: **Swifty**

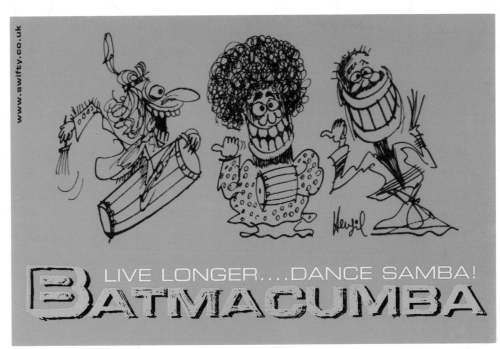

designed by: **Swifty**

designed by: **Swifty**

BATMACUMBA
THE 2001 SEASON: NOW EVEN SEXIER !

designed by: **Swifty**

designed by: **Swifty**

designed by: **Swifty**

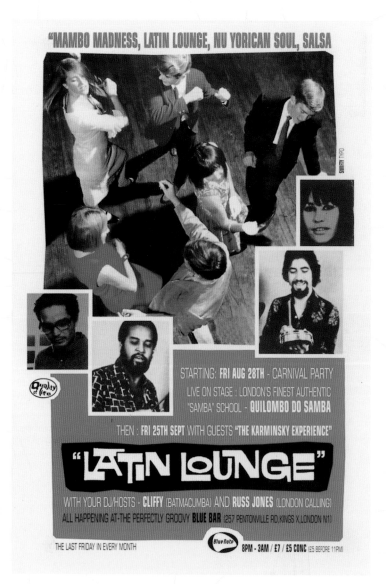

designed by: **Swifty**

"MAMBO MADNESS, LATIN LOUNGE, NU YORICAN SOUL, SALSA

"LATIN LOUNGE"

JOIN YOUR DJ/HOSTS -
CLIFFY (BATMACUMBA) & RUSS JONES (LONDON CALLING)
8PM - 3AM / £6/£4 CONC /FREE B4 9 / £4 B4 10
ALL HAPPENING AT-THE PERFECTLY GROOVY **CROSS BAR** (FORMERLY BLUE BAR)

MONTHLY FRIDAYS - JAN 22ND / FEB 26TH / MARCH 26TH. (257 PENTONVILLE RD,KINGS X,LONDON N1)

designed by: **Swifty**

designed by: **Swifty**

designed by: **Swifty**

hIP hOP

ARTWORKS BY: ANDREW RAE, PAUL ALLEN, BEN SWIFT, SHARP,
HEAVYWEIGHT, PARRA, PHIL REES, MR JAGO, DAVE KINSEY.

Dayglo Presents: ALL-DAYER WITH DE LA SOUL

CANDY FLIP
KICKING BACK
DEMON BOYZ
SHUT UP & DANCE
M.C. Mello
DADDY FREDDY + TENOR FLY
A Man Called Adam.

M.C. CARL COX
Paul Anderson
NORMAN COOK
FABIO
Trevor Fung
WILDCHILD
Marvin Connors
PAUL CLARKE

SUNDAY 24 JUNE
2PM—11PM
BRIGHTON CENTRE
Tickets £15 Box Office (0273) 202881

*author unknown

designed by: **Andrew Rae**

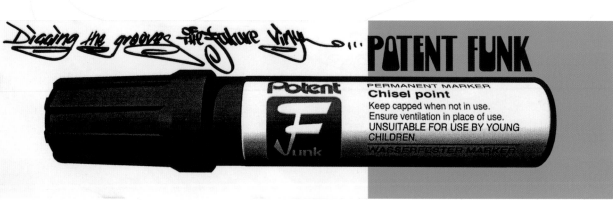

author unknown

Music by Ballistic Brothers, Sisters & Friends

Punk rock, new wave soul, pop music, salsa, rock n roll, calypso, reggae, rhythm & blues, master mix those number one tunes, "you pay at the door as a donation to hear the best sounds in creation". Doors open at 10pm- 5am. £8 & £6 conc. 3rd Friday of every month. Launch July 19th, August 16th, September 20th. The Blue Note, 1 Hoxton Square, London N1 6NU. Nearest tube: Old Street, limited parking.

designed by: **Paul Allen**

STANDTALL PRESENT:

ASHAWORLD MOVEMENT
DA N°1 SOUND OF LONDON
GOLDFINGER 'N' CHRIS FROM KISS FM

RAGGASONIC
DADDY MORY ET BIG RED
SOIRÉE ANIMÉE DÈS 22H30
PAR TERROR SEB

13 MAI D/AT STADIUM
66 AVE D'IVRY Ⓜ PORTE D'IVRY 🚌 PC62
PAF: 100F. NANAS GRATOS AV/MINUIT

designed by: **Mode2**

designed by: **Ben Swift**

ROCKERS REVENGE

HIP-HOP JAM IN HOXTON SQUARE: REVENGE AT LAST. WHO SAID IT WAS SWEET?

Blue Dot™ carhartt™

designed by: **Sharp**

BARNSTORMERS vs. HEAVYWEIGHT   MUSIC BY: DJ RICH MEDINA DEC.14

designed by: **Heavyweight**

August 16-17, 2002
HEAVYWEIGHT at ROPEADOPE

designed by: **Heavyweight**

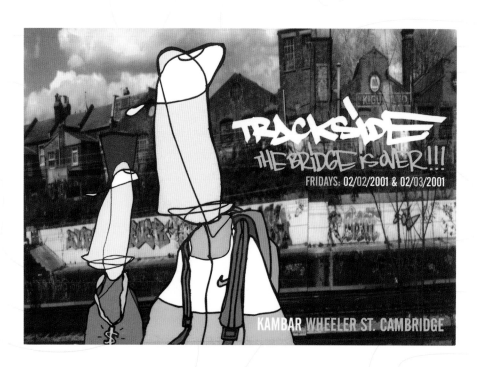

designed by: **Ben Swift**

designed by: **Ben Swift**

designed by: **Ben Swift**

designed by: **Ben Swift**

Chocolate©

BLACK EYED PEAS

31.08.2000 LIVE AT THE MELKWEG. Also called Cow Peas. Originating in Asia, the black-eyed pea is thought to have been introduced to the United States through the African slave trade. This small kidney-shaped bean has a black circular "eye" at its inner curve.

designed by: **Parra**

DEKEFEX PRESENTS...

THE SUNDAY
BREAKS

AN ALL DAY FEAST OF FUNK & FOOD
SUNDAY 11TH MARCH 2001

cargo 83 RIVINGTON STREET SHOREDITCH LONDON EC2
4PM-12MIDNITE EVERY 2ND SUNDAY OF THE MONTH FREE BEFORE 5PM £3 BEFORE 7PM £5 AFTER. 5 MINS. FROM OLD ST. TUBE TEL: 020 7739 3440   11*03*01

DEKEFEX PRESENTS...

THE SUNDAY
BREAKS

AN ALL DAY FEAST OF FUNK & FOOD
SUNDAY 8TH APRIL 2001

cargo 83 RIVINGTON STREET SHOREDITCH LONDON EC2 WWW.CARGO-LONDON.COM   8*04*01
4PM-12MIDNITE EVERY 2ND SUNDAY OF THE MONTH FREE B4 5PM £3 B4 7PM £5 AFTER 5 MINS. FROM OLD ST. TUBE TEL: 020 7739 3440

designed by: **Ben Swift**

designed by: **Azlan** - illustration by: **Mr Jago**

designed by: **Azlan** - illustration by: **Mr Jago**

designed by: **Dave Kinsey**

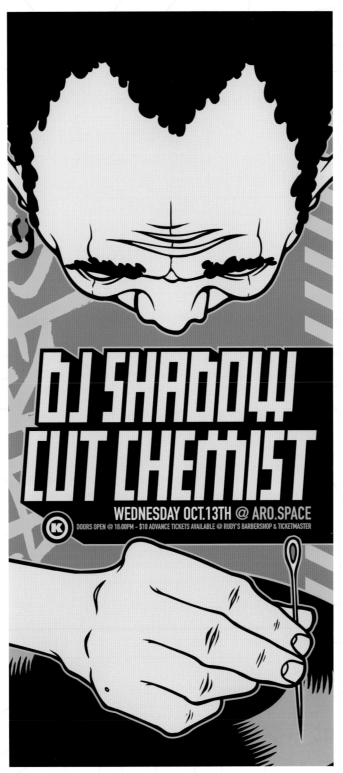

designed by: **Dave Kinsey**

series

ARTWORKS BY: SWIFTY, TOM HINGSTON. RAFFINERIE, GARETH BAYLISS, MAT, AUTOMAT, ALI AUGUR, HEAVYWEIGHT, LEO ELSTOB.

designed by: **Swifty**

designed by: **Swifty**

RESIDENT DJ'S - GILLES PETERSON / JAMES LAVELLE / BEN WILCOX

GUEST DJ'S (OCT/NOV '97) . 6TH OCTOBER-
DAVID HOLMES / 13TH OCTOBER - ROSS ALLEN
20TH OCTOBER-RAW DEAL / 27TH OCTOBER-
ROSS ALLEN / 3RD NOVEMBER-PAUL MARTIN
17TH NOVEMBER-PRESSURE DROP
EVERY MONDAY 10.30PM TILL 3.30AM

BAR RUMBA. 36 SHAFTESBURY AVENUE, LONDON W1 £3

THATS HOW IT IS!

©BAD BULL GRAFIX

THATS HOW IT IS!
Guest djs : July 98
6th July - Roni Size
13th July - Ross Allen

RESIDENT DJ'S - GILLES PETERSON / BEN WILCOX

EVERY MONDAY 10.30PM TILL 3.30AM. £3   BAR RUMBA 36 SHAFTESBURY AVENUE, LONDON W1

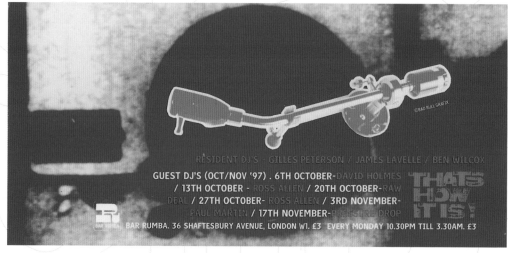

RESIDENT DJ'S - GILLES PETERSON / JAMES LAVELLE / BEN WILCOX

GUEST DJ'S (OCT/NOV '97) . 6TH OCTOBER-DAVID HOLMES
/ 13TH OCTOBER - ROSS ALLEN 20TH OCTOBER-RAW
DEAL / 27TH OCTOBER- ROSS ALLEN 3RD NOVEMBER-
PAUL MARTIN 17TH NOVEMBER-PRESSURE DROP
BAR RUMBA. 36 SHAFTESBURY AVENUE, LONDON W1. £3 EVERY MONDAY 10.30PM TILL 3.30AM. £3

THATS HOW IT IS!

©BAD BULL GRAFIX

designed by: **Swifty**

THATS HOW IT IS!

Guest djs : July 98
6th July – Roni Size / 13th July – Ross Allen

RESIDENT DJ'S - GILLES PETERSON / BEN WILCOX
EVERY MONDAY 10.30PM TILL 3.30AM. £3   BAR RUMBA 36 SHAFTESBURY AVENUE, LONDON W1

RESIDENT DJ'S - GILLES PETERSON / JAMES LAVELLE / BEN WILCOX

GUEST DJ'S (OCT/NOV '97) . 6TH OCTOBER-DAVID HOLMES / 13TH OCTOBER - ROSS ALLEN / 20TH OCTOBER-RAW DEAL / 27TH OCTOBER- ROSS ALLEN / 3RD NOVEMBER-PAUL MARTIN / 17TH NOVEMBER-PRESSURE DROP

THATS HOW IT IS!

BAR RUMBA 36 SHAFTESBURY AVENUE, LONDON W1   EVERY MONDAY 10.30PM TILL 3.30AM. £3

THATS HOW IT IS!

Guest djs : July 98
6th July – Roni Size
13th July – Ross Allen

RESIDENT DJ'S - GILLES PETERSON / BEN WILCOX
EVERY MONDAY 10.30PM TILL 3.30AM. £3   BAR RUMBA 36 SHAFTESBURY AVENUE, LONDON W1

designed by: **Swifty**

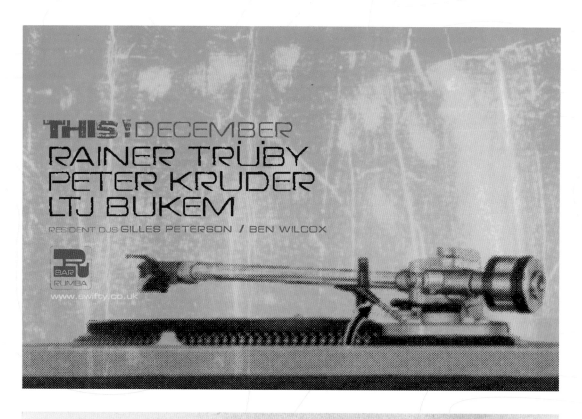

THIS! DECEMBER
RAINER TRÜBY
PETER KRUDER
LTJ BUKEM
RESIDENT DJS GILLES PETERSON / BEN WILCOX

BAR RUMBA
www.swifty.co.uk

THIS!
RAW DEAL / DEGO (4 HERO)
ZED BIAS / MATTHEW HERBERT
special guest dj's sept 2001 a month of madness!
THIS!

designed by: **Swifty**

THIS :OCTOBER
ALEX ATTIAS
REPRAZENT
KYOTO JAZZ MASSIVE
ASHLEY BEADLE
RESIDENT DJS GILLES PETERSON / BEN WILCOX

designed by: **Swifty**

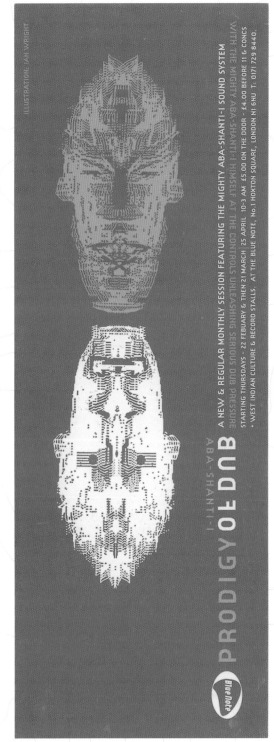

designed by: **Tom Hingston** - illustration by: **Ian Wright**

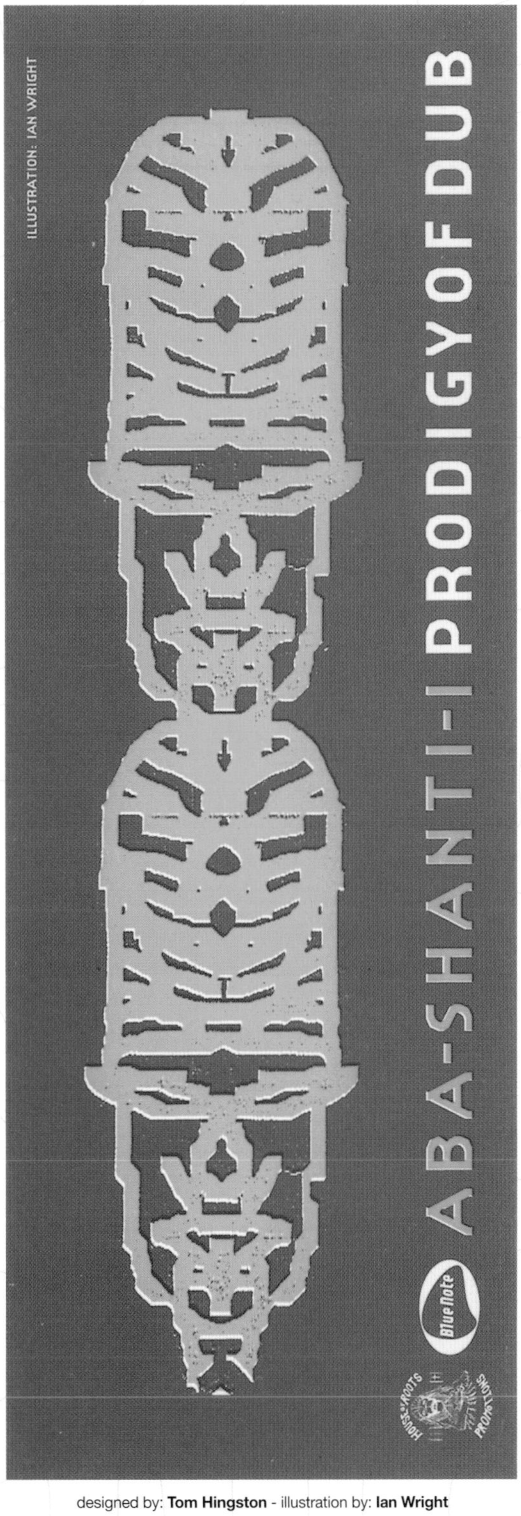

ILLUSTRATION: IAN WRIGHT

ABA-SHANTI-I PRODIGY OF DUB

Blue Note

designed by: **Tom Hingston** - illustration by: **Ian Wright**

GILLES PETERSON, BEN WILCOX, PAUL BRADSHAW & GUESTS ✈ FAR EAST

GILLES PETERSON, BEN WILCOX, PAUL BRADSHAW & GUESTS ✈ FAR EAST

designed by: **Tom Hingston**

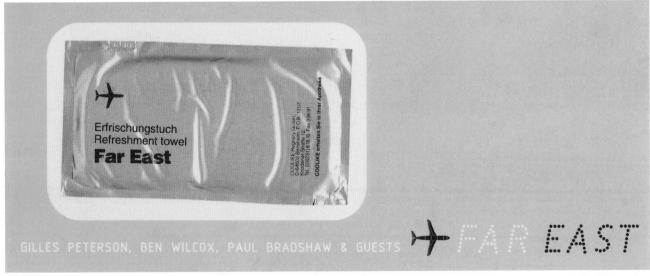

designed by: **Tom Hingston**

Fr.12.01.01 alex dallas & alex gustafson (earthbound)
gianni siravo & roberto ceschi (sequel)
straight ahead im seebad enge ab 23.00 (bei tramhaltestelle rentenanstalt am see)
futuristische und innovative beats in einem beheizten raum.

26.01.01 straight ahead präsentieren
HIDDEN AGENDA & ALEX DALLAS
kommt und tanzt mit uns im seebad enge (bei tramhaltestelle rentenanstalt am see)
dem beheizten club für nu jazzheadz, brokenbeatniks & one love clubbers (ab 23.00h)

02.02.01 straight ahead präsentieren die plattentaufe von
SEQUEL feat. gianni siravo & roberto ceschi
kommt und tanzt mit uns im seebad enge (bei tramhaltestelle rentenanstalt am see)
dem beheizten club für nu jazzheadz, brokenbeatniks & one love clubbers (ab 23.00h)

designed by: **Raffinerie**

Fr. 23.03.01 stephane attias (visions, laws of motion, lausanne)
alex dallas (earthbound)
straight ahead präsentiert eine nacht mit brockenbeatz, phusion, nu jazz + electric soul
SEEBAD ENGE (bei tramhaltestelle rentenanstalt am see) ab 23.00h
für sms-infos über straight ahead: kennwort AHEAD an Zielnummer 266 senden.

Sa.10.03.01 alex gustafson (earthbound)
gianni siravo (sequel)
kommt und tanzt mit uns im seebad enge (bei tramhaltestelle rentenanstalt am see)
dem beheizten club für nu jazzheadz, brokenbeatniks & one love clubbers (ab 23.00h)

Fr.13.4.01 sequel + alex dallas (earthbound)
Fr.20.4.01 nico canzoniere << freeform arkestra earthbound >>>>> **alex gustafson**
straight ahead präsentiert eine nacht mit brockenbeatz, phusion, nu jazz + electric soul
SEEBAD ENGE (bei tramhaltestelle rentenanstalt am see) ab 23.00h
für sms-infos über straight ahead: kennwort AHEAD an Zielnummer 266 senden.

designed by: **Raffinerie**

STRAIGHT AHEAD
RECORDINGS
PRESENTS:
ONE STEP AHEAD - RELEASE PARTY
SONNTAG, 18. JULI 1999 AB 21.00 H

STRAIGHT AHEAD DJS:
ALEX DALLAS
(EARTHBOUND)_
SEQUEL
FREEFORM ARKESTRA
AND VERY SPECIALGUESTS:

GILLES PETERSON
(TALKIN' LOUD) LONDON

CHARLIE DARK
(ATTICA BLUES_ABSENT MINDED)

RAW DEAL
(TALKIN' LOUD) LONDON

HIDDEN AGENDA
(METALHEADZ)

JONY ROCKSTAR
NAKED FUNK (PUSSYFOOT RECORDS)

AUF DREI FLOORS
THEATERSAAL HOFKULT+
OPEN-AIR CHILL OUT
KAUFLEUTEN
PELIKANSTR. 18
8001 ZÜRICH

designed by: **Raffinerie**

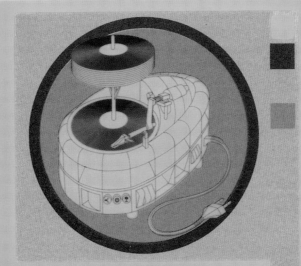

STRAIGHT AHEAD
RECORDINGS
PRESENTS:
ONE STEP AHEAD - RELEASE PARTY
SONNTAG, 18. JULI 1999 AB 21.00 H

STRAIGHT AHEAD DJS:
ALEX DALLAS
(EARTHBOUND)
SEQUEL
FREEFORM ARKESTRA
AND VERY SPECIAL GUESTS:

GILLES PETERSON
(TALKIN' LOUD) LONDON

CHARLIE DARK
(ATTICA BLUES _ ABSENT MINDED)

RAW DEAL
(TALKIN' LOUD) LONDON

HIDDEN AGENDA
(METALHEADS)

JONY ROCKSTAR
NAKED FUNK (PUSSYFOOT RECORDS)

AUF DREI FLOORS
THEATERSAAL · HOFKLUB +
OPEN-AIR CHILL OUT
KAUFLEUTEN
PELIKANSTR. 18
8001 ZÜRICH

designed by: **Raffinerie**

HONEST ION'S RECORDS
THE BIG BAR
AT THE CRYPT ST. MATTHEWS CHURCH
BRIXTON SW2 SEVEN UNTIL LATE
FIFTEENTH OF MAY 2002
RESIDENT DJS MARK AINLEY WILL BANKHEAD
DJ KOOL TETSU LIL' TOBY AND EMMET KEANE
FREE BEFORE EIGHT THREE POUNDS THEREAFTER

designed by: **Gareth Bayliss**

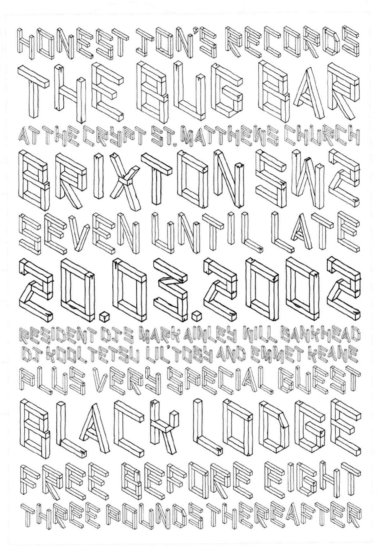

designed by: **Gareth Bayliss**

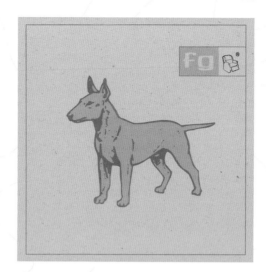

designed by: **mat**

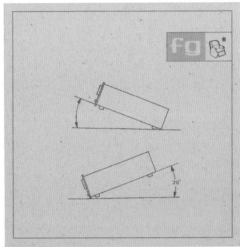

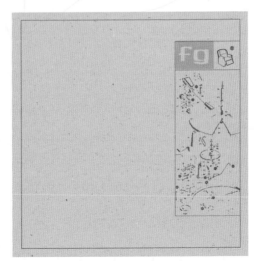

designed by: **mat**

■ Automat-Label-Night 11.04.02. 21:00 Club-U Künstlerhauspassage

⊠ AUTOMAT

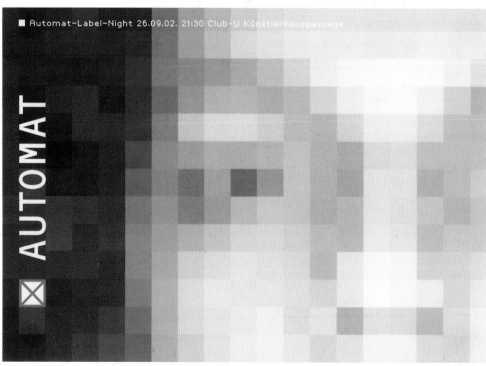

■ Automat-Label-Night 26.09.02. 21:30 Club-U Künstlerhauspassage

AUTOMAT ⊠

designed by: **Automat**

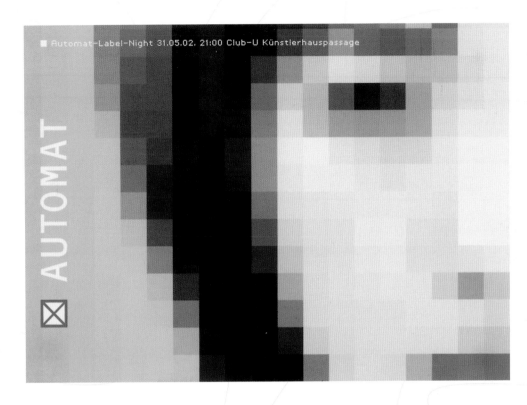

■ Automat-Label-Night 31.05.02. 21:00 Club-U Künstlerhauspassage

AUTOMAT

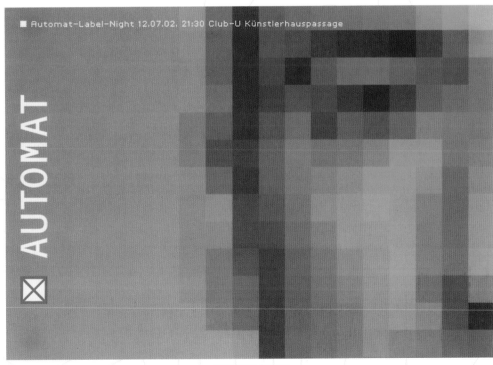

■ Automat-Label-Night 12.07.02. 21:30 Club-U Künstlerhauspassage

AUTOMAT

designed by: **Automat**

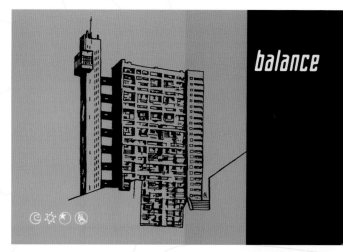

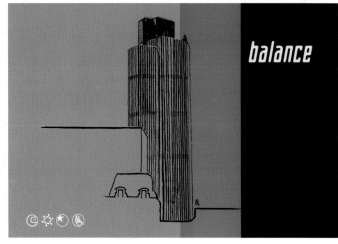

designed by: **Ali Augur**

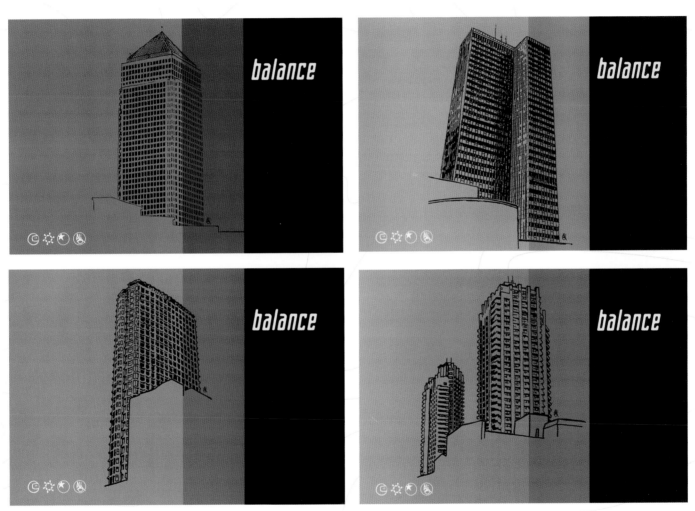

designed by: **Ali Augur**

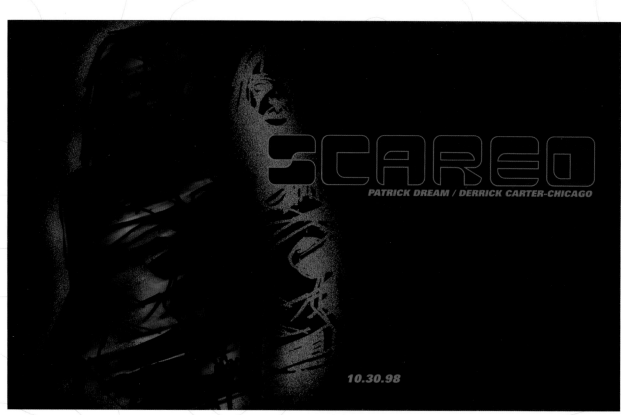

SCARED
PATRICK DREAM / DERRICK CARTER-CHICAGO

10.30.98

designed by: **Heavyweight**

designed by: **Heavyweight**

designed by: **Leo Elstob**

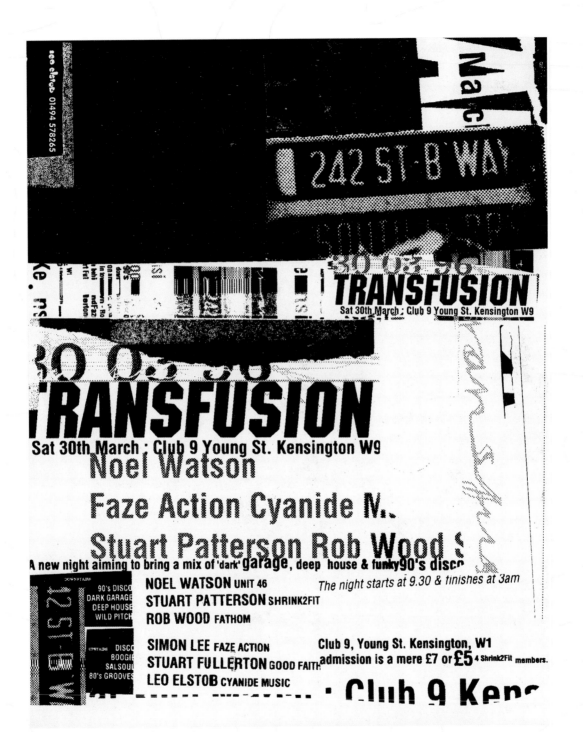

TRANSFUSION
Sat 30th March : Club 9 Young St. Kensington W9

TRANSFUSION
Sat 30th March : Club 9 Young St. Kensington W9

Noel Watson

Faze Action Cyanide M..

Stuart Patterson Rob Wood $

A new night aiming to bring a mix of 'dark' garage, deep house & funky 90's disco

90's DISCO
DARK GARAGE
DEEP HOUSE
WILD PITCH

DISCO
BOOGIE
SALSOUL
80's GROOVES

NOEL WATSON UNIT 46
STUART PATTERSON SHRINK2FIT
ROB WOOD FATHOM

SIMON LEE FAZE ACTION
STUART FULLERTON GOOD FAITH
LEO ELSTOB CYANIDE MUSIC

The night starts at 9.30 & finishes at 3am

Club 9, Young St. Kensington, W1
admission is a mere £7 or £5 4 Shrink2Fit members.

Club 9 Kens

designed by: **Leo Elstob**

*author unknown

*author unknown

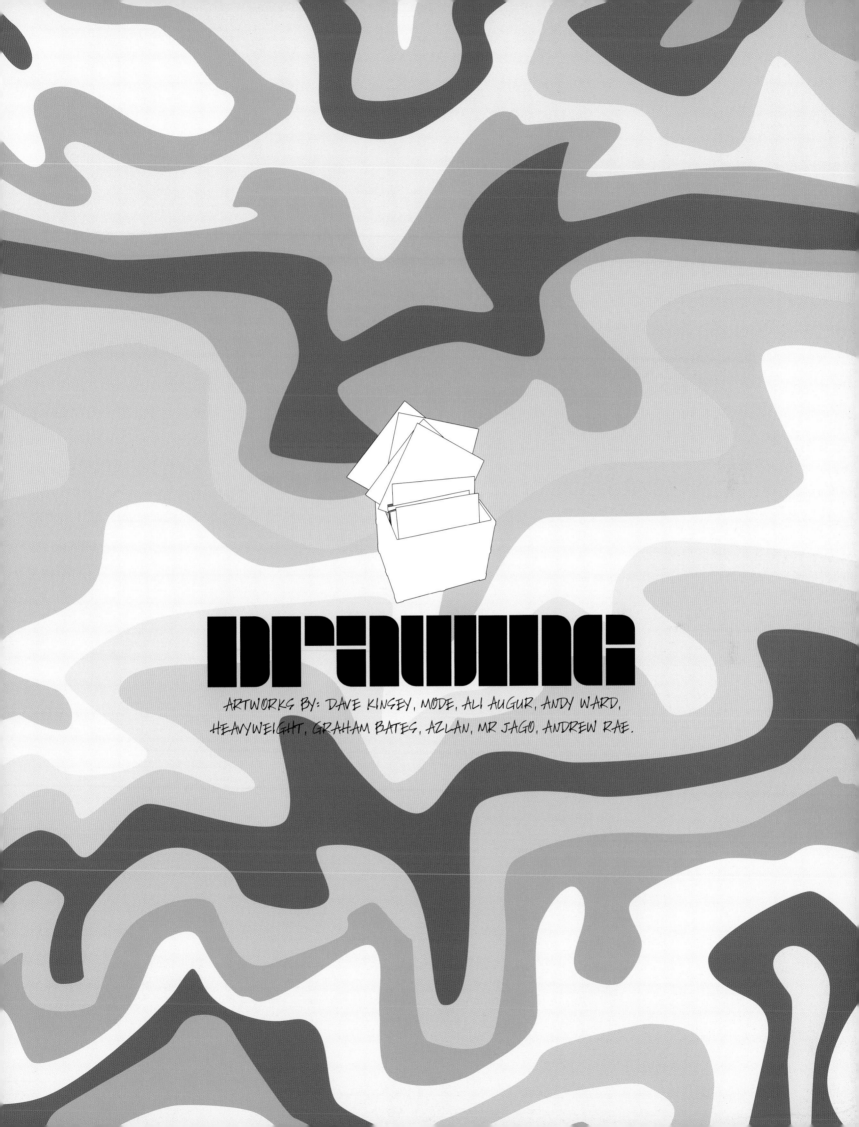

DRAWING

ARTWORKS BY: DAVE KINSEY, MODE, ALI AUGUR, ANDY WARD,
HEAVYWEIGHT, GRAHAM BATES, AZLAN, MR JAGO, ANDREW RAE.

designed by: **Swifty** - illustration by: **Mode2**

The Justice League presents..

JEAN-JACQUES PERREY

LIVE LECTURE/DEMONSTRATION
WEDNESDAY OCTOBER 21ST 1998 > 8PM - 10PM
@ The Justice League 628 Divisadero at Hayes
ADMISSION $7.00
At 10PM, PAWS-A-TIVITY (HIP-HOP, SOUL & DANCE HALL) with DJ-PAWS & J.BOOGIE
FOR MORE INFO. CALL>415.440.0409

designed by: **Dave Kinsey**

designed by: **Graham Bates**

designed by: **Graham Bates**

DJ Craze + Krust

DMC World Mixing Champion

Knowledge & popwire.com
present a hip hop. drum & bass and breaks spectacular
Thursday 20th April @ Cafe Blue. Bristol

KNOWLEDGE® DRUM & BASS / HIP-HOP / BREAKS / STREET CULTURE + popwire.com® 'short cut to new music'

designed by: **Azlan** - illustration by: **Mr Jago**

scratch some sessions

designed by: **Azlan** - illustration by: **Mr Jago**

designed by: **Andy Ward**

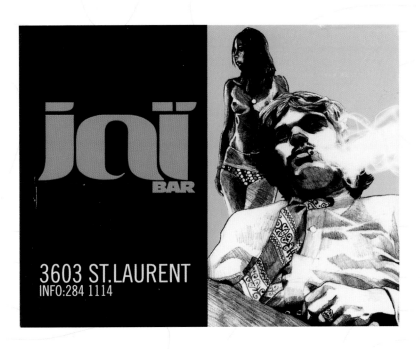

designed by: **Heavyweight**

designed by: **Ali Augur**

designed by: **Ali Augur**

designed by: **Ali Augur**

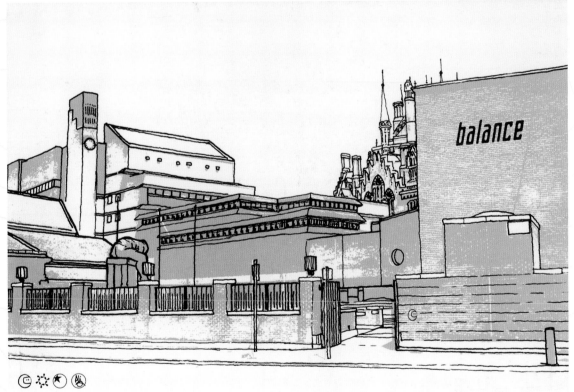

designed by: **Ali Augur**

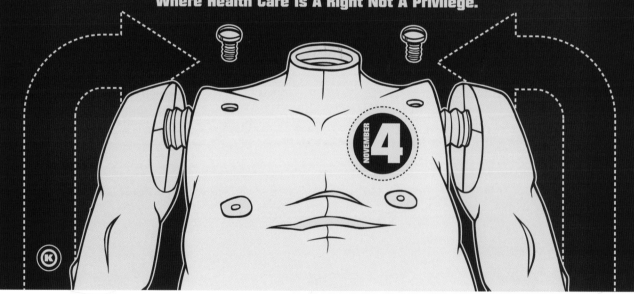

designed by: **Dave Kinsey**

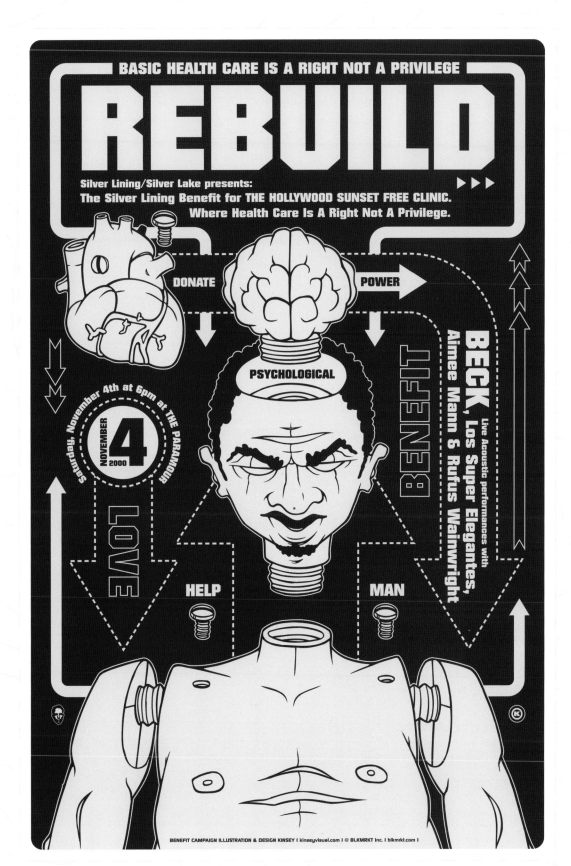

designed by: **Dave Kinsey**

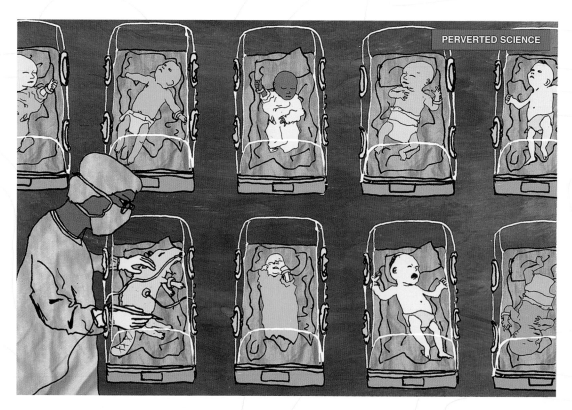

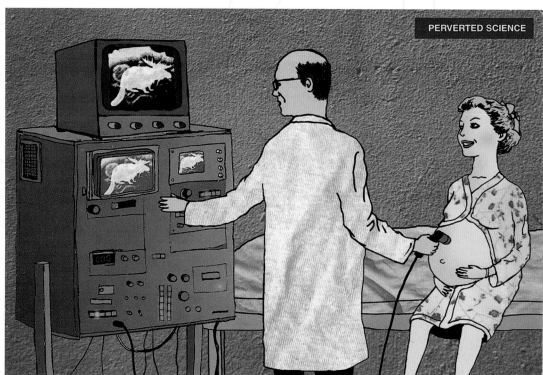

designed by: **Andrew Rae**

designed by: **Andrew Rae**

1ST STEPS

1ST PADDLE

1ST BIRTHDAY

1ST CAKE

1ST MARSHMALLOW

1ST BLOOD

designed by: **Andrew Rae**

designed by: **Andrew Rae**

Perverted Science

designed by: **Andrew Rae**

designed by: **Andrew Rae**

designed by: **Andrew Rae**

designed by: **Andrew Rae**

designed by: **Andrew Rae**

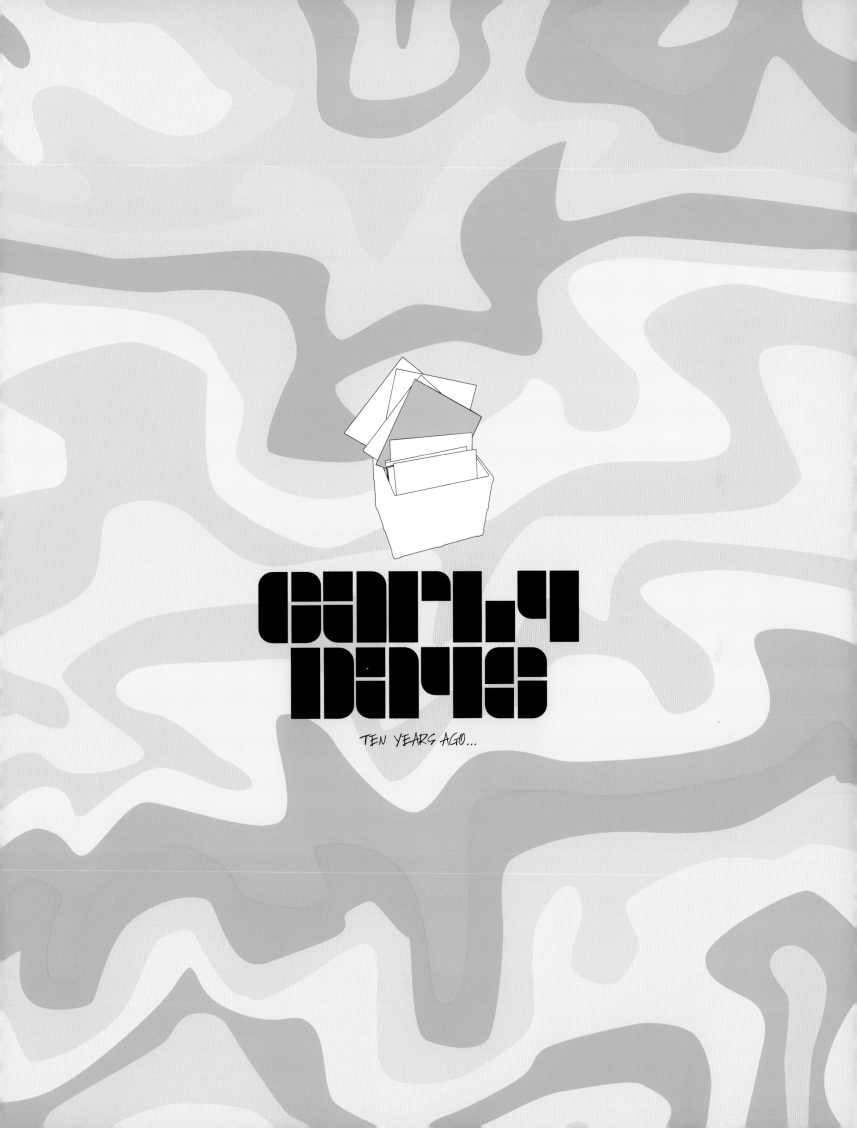

CURLY DAYS

TEN YEARS AGO...

STARTING AUG 1ST...
RECKLESS
RECORDS »

AT WOODY'S Woodfield Road, W9.

↑UPSTAIRS

"WEIRD · FUNK"
— THE DANCE MUSICS EXPLORED!

djs
SEAN P. & BIBI

DOWNSTAIRS ↓

"REAL HOUSE"

CHICAGO · N.Y. · DETROIT

djs
ZAF & KIRK

10 til 3am Every Thursday Night
Entrance to the Underground £5
Info; 071 437 4271.
071 359 0501

Talkin Loud & Saying Something 3rd Anniversary meets Straight No Chaser to present

Dave Valentin Quintet
Numero Uno Latin Jazz flautist - 4pm
The Courtney Pine All Stars
Jam session stylee - 7pm
PA's: Kid Frost + Galliano
DJs Gilles Peterson & Patrick Forge

£7 on Door (£5 for members)

Sunday, 2nd December 1990. 1am to 9pm Dingwalls Camden Lock, NW1 (071. 267 4967)

designed by: **Swifty**

TALKIN' LOUD
AND SAYING SOMETHING
AT DINGWALLS

DJ's: THE ORIGINAL CREW;
GILLES PETERSON & PATRICK FORGE
TALKIN LOUD & DINGWALLS REUNION MEMBERS
£4/£5 OTHERS
SUNDAY 6TH JUNE 1993
START: **12 MIDDAY** - REMEMBER ON THE DOT
FINISH: **7.00PM**

Summer sunshine is on it's way and life is looking sweet with the monthly session of **Talkin' Loud and Saying Something** returning on **Sunday 6th June**. It's been hard to believe but I can quite honestly say that the vibe is as strong now as it was back in the early days of Talkin' Loud and Saying Something. Now I know there will be cynics out there who will not believe, but believe what you see, the vibe is strong, loud and very sound.

Remember the bar shuts at 3pm, the doors open at midday and early arrival is still the only real guarantee of entry.

There will be a **live band** but unfortunately I'm not allowed to say due to a publicity thang! but it will be firing all the way. So with a crisp sound system, Brazilian rhythms in abundance, seven hours of severe sounds and the chance to hit the market whenever, life will be sweet and joyful on a **Dingwalls Sunday afternoon.**

For those that remember, for those that wished they'd been there, it doesn't really matter as long as you are there.
Gilles & Patrick

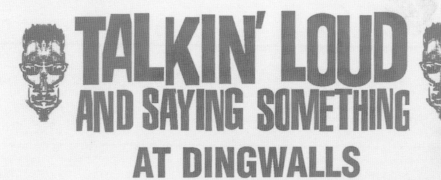

TALKIN' LOUD
AND SAYING SOMETHING
AT DINGWALLS

DJ's: THE ORIGINAL CREW;
GILLES PETERSON & PATRICK FORGE
TALKIN LOUD & DINGWALLS REUNION MEMBERS
£4/£5 OTHERS
SUNDAY 2ND MAY 1993
START: 12 MIDDAY - REMEMBER ON THE DOT
FINISH: 7PM ISH!

Easter Sunday's session at the new Dingwalls really proved that
Talkin' Loud and Saying Something is back with a vengence. A crisp
sound system, families in abundance, Brazilian rhythms flowing,
seven hours of Jazz indulgence on a Sunday afternoon!
So the good news is the session returns on **Sunday May 2nd** to
coincide with the Bank Holiday. Remember the bar shuts at 3pm, the
doors open at midday and early arrival is still the only real guarantee
of entry.
Live music is from **Secret Society** with their distinctive brand of
Mancunian Jazz poetics. Don't forget that once you're inside
Dingwalls you can visit the market whenever and due to the success
of opening til 7pm, we're doing it again.

Talkin' Loud & Saying Something, as always, a family affair!

For those that remember, for those that wished they'd been there, it
doesn't really matter as long as you are there.
Gilles & Patrick

THE DEViL'S DEN

presents real soul and rare grooves

Sat, March 9th at Vino Veritas [formerly the Cask & Glass]
23 Orchard St, W1 [off Oxford St, behind M & S] 9pm-2am
DJs Ivor Jones, Ian Clark & Gary Dennis £5.00 in advance

for tickets &
information
tel 0181 573 9224

*author unknown

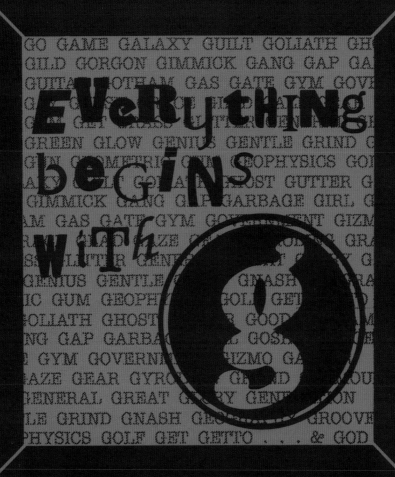

GOODENOUGH 20th CENTURY

10.30pm THURSDAYS 1992
APPLE TREE YARD (OFF DUKE OF YORK ST.) PICADILLY SW1

SAM BULLY · MICHAEL KOPELMAN · ALEX BABY · RICHARD BRESLAW
MOVIES BY : *CRUNCH* · MARK LEBON, *FILMS* · JAMES LEBON

designed by: **Masaki**

*author unknown

SHAKE YER WIG!

AT THE JAZZ ROOMS
(10 SHIP STREET)

SOUL	RAP
RARE	JAZZ
FUNK	RAGGA

EVERY WEDNESDAY
10PM - 2AM
ADMISSION £3/£2 CONC.

*author unknown

jazz 90

9pm
till late

£3.50
with this
leaflet

On : Sat 24th Feb 1990 At : The Emerald
Centre,Hammersmith (On the roundabout next to the
tube st) Music : Down the line ....Hard Core
DJ's : Sylvester and Gilles Peterson.

jazz 90

9.30 pm
till late

£5.00
with this
leaflet
£6 on door

On : Sat 17th Nov 1990 At : The Emerald
Centre,Hammersmith (On the roundabout next to the
tube st) Music : Down the line ....Hard Core
DJ's : Sylvester and Gilles Peterson.

designed by: **Swifty**

SUMMER SPLASH '92

PROUDLY PRESENTS
Batty Rider & Sportswear
.THE HEAT. PART 1
15th AUGUST 1992
AT
BLACK NATION SOCIAL CLUB
107d DOWNS RD
CLAPTON E5
(opposite Mingles wine bar)

YOU WILL BE PASSIONATELY ENTERTAINED BY:

BLACK NATION MOVEMENT

PLUS FULL GHETTO SWING CREW

☀ AROUND THE CONTROL TOWER ☀

BIG FINGER - DANGERMAN - PABLO RANKS

MANAGEMENT :- SOLO DAN

FREE CHAMPAGNE RAFFLE

LADIES SAFE B - 4 - 1

☎ BLACK NATION HOTLINE : BUSES: 253, S2, 38
0831 182613   BRITISH RAIL*
CLAPTON STATION

Design by Graphfix 0992-660323

author unknown

COLDSWEAT PRODUCTIONS PRESENTS

"BOOGALOO" VILLAGE

BANDS	DJ'S
	UPSTAIRS
C-PHUNKAPHOBIA	ABBI FREEMAN
(Featuring MARK CHI)	CAV
and	BRIAN NORMAN
	PATRICK DOWNSTAIRS
?	RONNIE
***	+
	COLDSWEAT'S CREW

FASHION DISPLAY

CONGO BASS SHOW THEIR LATEST DESIGNS

SOUL KITCHEN

RICE AND PEAS AND CHICKEN
AVAILABLE

MONDAY 2ND MARCH 1992
10 - 3
ENTRANCE £5.00

136 SHAFTSBURY AVENUE. W. 1.

author unknown

TOUCH BASS PRESENTS

HOUSE PARTY

Professional Venue

ON CARNIVAL WEEKEND

ON SATURDAY 29th/SUNDAY 30th CARNIVAL
WEEKEND THERE WILL BE A HOUSE PARTY FROM

10p.m-6a.m at:-

Basement floor+Large Raised Garden
9 Aldridge Road Villas,London,W11-1BL
(The entrance to the House Party is down the side)
HOUSE/HIP-HOP/SOUL/RAGGA+MORE
Special attractions:-GUEST DJ`s,BAR+FOOD
ALL NIGHT,LASER/STROBELIGHTS,TURBO
SOUND SYSTEM.£5 PER PERSON ON THE DOOR.
Nearest tube station:-Westbourne Park Station.

*author unknown

PROGRESSION
EVERY FRIDAY
at
The silver Lady 386 West Green Rd N16
Turnpike lane

£3   8pm-2am   £3

Resident Ruff Crew DJ's on rotation

 TC
HOUSEMAN
ENAAGEE
HAMISH

and forthcoming confirmed guests

JEFF(spiral tribe)

ZU(Wetback,Cornwall)

CAMDEN(Drum club)

ALEX(Fat Cat Records)

TERROREYES(Spiral,Knowledge)

Ruff crew have been DJing for over 3 years with involvement in Spiral Tribe
Wetback(Cornwall),Techno productions(Paris),Rockshots(Newcastle),Prism
(Oxford),Touchdown 94.1fm(London)plus many more on the vibe kind of tings

*author unknown

HALLOWEEN
SATURDAY OCT. 30TH
HOUSE  NATION

INVITES YOU TO EXPERTENCE
THE SOUNDS OF NY'S PREMIERE DJ'S

TIMMY & DAVID
RICAHARDSON   MORALES
622 BROADWAY
BET. BLEECKER & HOUSTON
DOORS OPEN MIDNITE
STAY LATE!

DONATION
LADIES: $5 w/INVITE B4 2AM
GENTS: $7 w/INVITE B4 2AM

PLENTY OF FOOD
MUNCHIES & FRUIT
3 ROOMS OF DANCING

#6 & F TRAINS TO BWAY/LAFAYETTE•INFO...(718)789-6220
LOVE MAKES THE DAY...MUSIC MAKES THE NIGHT

author unknown

UNUSUAL SHAPE

ARTWORKS BY: RAFFINERIE, DANILO BETTONI

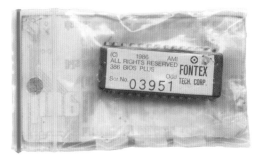

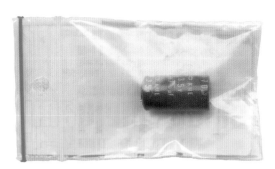

author unknown

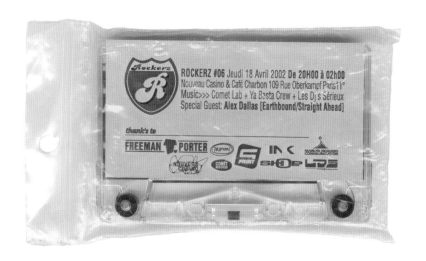

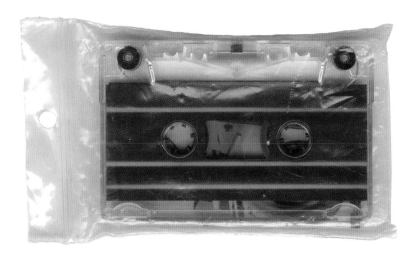

author unknown

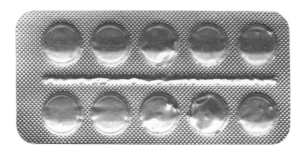

author unknown

slamjam orange mix > 281002

1 wanna be your lover - automan
bootleg - 2002

2 nights in berlin - daniel wang
environ - 2001

3 brennan green behind the ocean
balihu - 2002

4 delight frank roger & dj roy
straight up - 2001

5 evidence metro area
environ - 2002

6 finally - dj meri vox mix kings of tomorrow
defected - 2001

7 looking for love - original mix vikter duplaix
hollywood records - 2002

8 sunday descent - hakan libdo remix slockden project
straylight recordings - 2002

9 pure - petalpusher vocal blue six
naked music - 2000

10 simmer down - reel people remix every day people
papa records - 2002

selezione di giovanni de marchi

slamjam yellow mix > 111102

1 forever in my life - prince
bootleg 198?

2 let me go! instrumental - heaven 17
virgin 1982

3 when we were all together... - kelley polar quartet
environ 2002

4 ghost trains - erlend oye
source 2002

5 wardance - automan 4
bootleg 2002

6 when i'm with you - george levin
sonar kollektiv 2000

7 deep burnt - pepe bradock
kif 1999

8 julius papp - a thousand years
nite grooves 2002

9 qwerty - connective zone
emoticon 2002

10 solitary flight - theo parrish
flight sound 2002

selezione di giovanni de marchi

designed by: **Danilo Bettoni**

slamjam blue mix > 141002

1 nomad - dj nori
flower records 2001

2 brennan green - etc. whatever
balihu 2002

3 two tribes - frankie goes to hollywood
ztt 1984

4 intro/outro original mix - frankie valentine
sunshine enterprises 2002

5 harmony (dixon's late night mix) - at jazz
mantis recordings 2002

6 break it down - veena harlem
urbantorque 2002

7 gimme more - andreas greiner jr
fm music 2002

8 present pretense - john tejada
tiger sushi 2002

9 surrender - petalpusher
naked music 1999

10 we also not - metro area
tiger sushi 2002

selezione di giovanni de marchi

slamjam fucsia mix > 251102

1 surrender your love (mkl mix) - sade
bootleg 2002

2 runaway train - victor davies
jcr 2002

3 under your sky (intega rmx) - the undervolves
jcr 2002

4 easy life - son dexter
alleviated 2002

5 fade - solu music
wave music 2001

6 surrender - petalpusher
naked music 1999

7 things you do for me - modaji
papa 2002

8 space rider (spinna club mix) - shaun escoffrey
oyster 2002

9 mind expansions (blaze shelter mix) - kyoto jazz massive
compost 2002

10 white pony - laidback
sire records 1983

selezione di giovanni de marchi

designed by: **Danilo Bettoni**

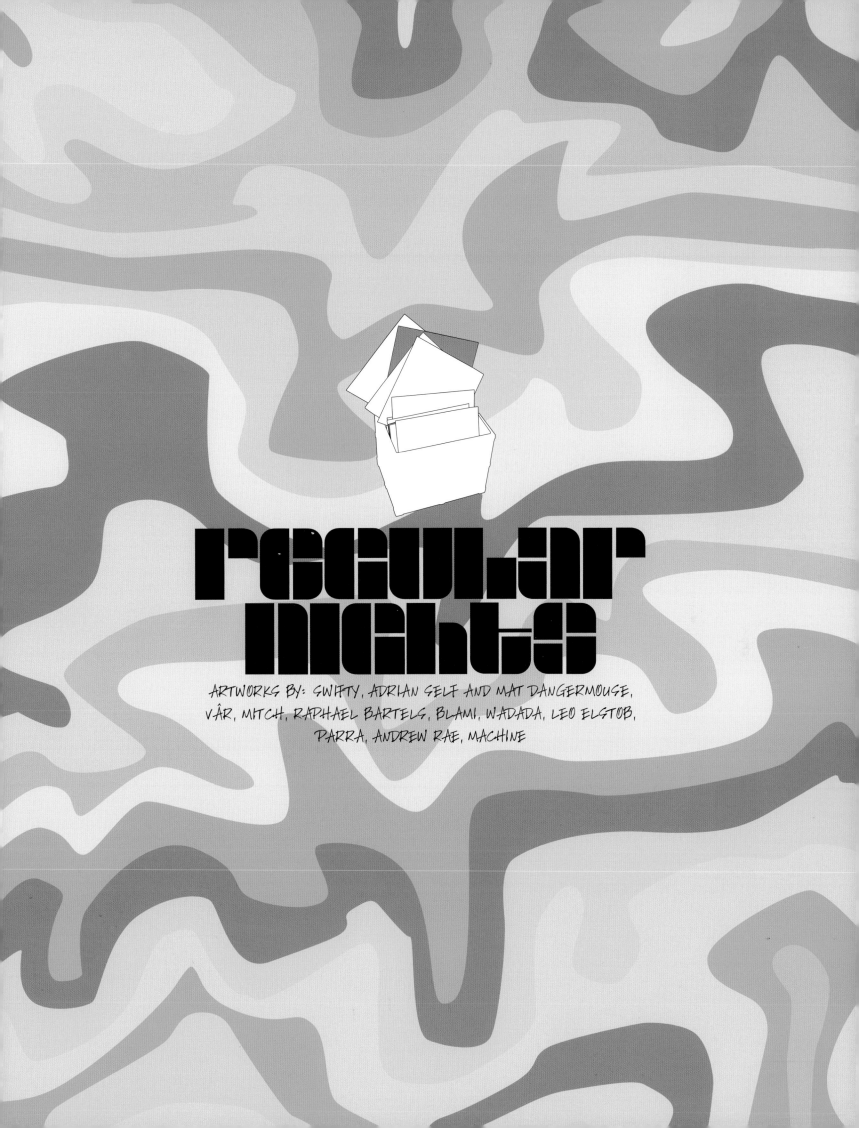

regular nights

ARTWORKS BY: SWIFTY, ADRIAN SELF AND MAT DANGERMOUSE,
VÂR, MITCH, RAPHAEL BARTELS, BLAMI, WADADA, LEO ELSTOB,
PARRA, ANDREW RAE, MACHINE

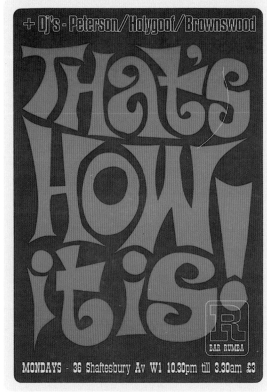

designed by: **Swifty**

designed by: **Swifty**

designed by: **Adrian Self & Mat Dangermouse**

DYNAMITE!

SKA · SOUL · ROCKSTEADY · FUNK · DUB

100%

designed by: **Adrian Self & Mat Dangermouse**

designed by: **Adrian Self & Mat Dangermouse**

designed by: **Adrian Self & Mat Dangermouse**

designed by: **Adrian Self & Mat Dangermouse**

designed by: **Adrian Self & Mat Dangermouse**

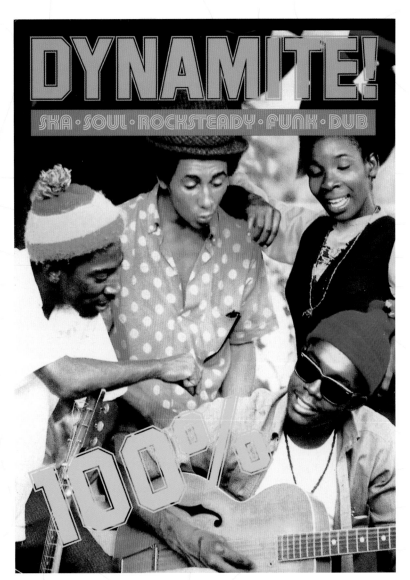

designed by: **Adrian Self & Mat Dangermouse**

designed by: **Adrian Self & Mat Dangermouse**

SOUL JAZZ RECORDS PRESENTS
NU YORICA!
LATIN·DISCO·SOUL·FUNK

THE SOUND OF NEW YORK

OPENING NIGHT
FRIDAY 19TH NOVEMBER
AT GOSSIPS NIGHTCLUB,
69 DEAN STREET,
LONDON W1
10-3AM £5
SOULJAZZSOUNDSYSTEM DJ'S

designed by: **Adrian Self & Mat Dangermouse**

NU YORICA!
LATIN·DISCO·FUNK·SOUL

SOULJAZZSOUNDSYSTEM DJ'S EVERY MONDAY
at the Notting Hill Arts Club, 21 Notting Hill Gate
7pm-1am £4/£3 concessions Free before 9.30pm

NU YORICA!
LATIN·DISCO·FUNK·SOUL

SOULJAZZSOUNDSYSTEM DJ'S EVERY MONDAY
at the Notting Hill Arts Club, 21 Notting Hill Gate
7pm-1am £4/£3 concessions Free before 9.30pm

designed by: **Adrian Self & Mat Dangermouse**

fusion en musikklubb på **sturecompagniet**
onsdag 26 juli kl 2130 till 0300
abstrakt deep house + varma new jersey grooves på stora golvet:

DJ YANNICK

needs production/tyskland + MAD MATS
jazzrummet:

LES GAMMAS

compost/tyskland + CLAES BODÉN + JONAS LÖNNÅ
entré 50 kr för alla. mer fusion på www.discosthlm.com
vi vill tacka vår, universal music och levi's engineered jeans

fusion i samarbete med levi's® engineered jeans ™ presenterar:

A FUSION SOUL CLASSICS COLLECTION

stor fest för **fusions soulsamling** onsdag 1 mars kl 21.30 till 03.00 på **sturecompagniet**
stora golvet: varm deephouse & garage med

FRANKIE VALENTINE london + jonas lönnå

jazzrummet: soulklassiker med:

DR BOB JONES london + mad mats + claes bodén

50 kr, 20 år. fusion med ovärderligt stöd från pripps blå, universal music, nöjesguiden, vår & mtv. kom i tid, de första hundra får fintfin fusionpresent
→ köp skivan a fusion soul classics collection från och med 3 mars i din skivbutik eller på
www.discosthlm.com/fusion där du även kan följa fusion i text och bild, lyssna på musiken och tävla.

en **musik**klubb. part 1 av volym 2 kl 21 till 03
onsdag 25 augusti Sturecompagniet + mad mats & claes bodén
fusiongolvet:

dj snowboy .uk + mad mats & claes bodén

nere: **london electricity** chris goss .uk + jonas lönnå
the rummet vår oordnar **vår04** / innehåller fu + dan jakob & kaell grammyaward & dj hockyfopell
entré 50 kr för alla. tillsammans med finnair & levi'st mer om fusion på www.discosthlm.com

designed by: **Vår**

designed by: **Vår**

designed by: **Mitch**

designed by: **Mitch**

designed by: **Mitch**

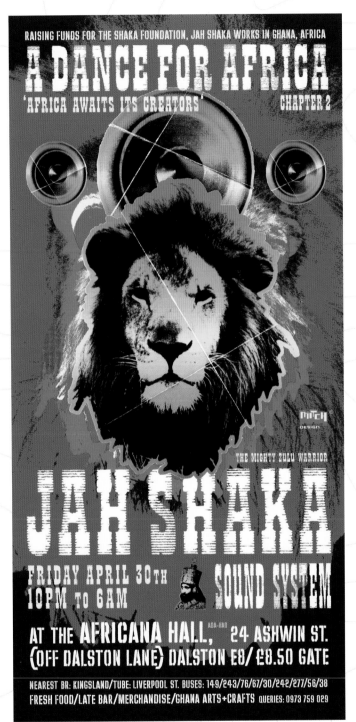

designed by: **Mitch**

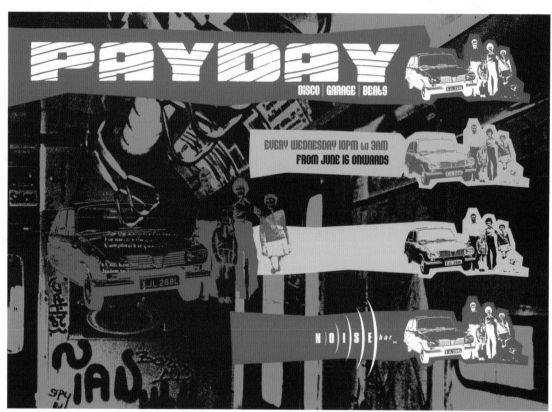

designed by: **Mitch**

designed by: **Mitch**

designed by: **Raphael Bartels**

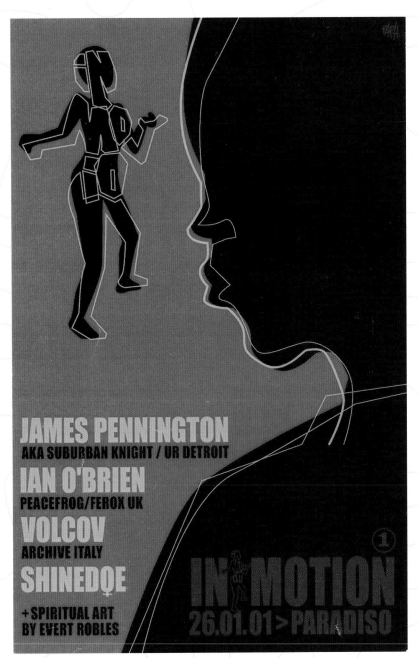

designed by: **Raphael Bartels**

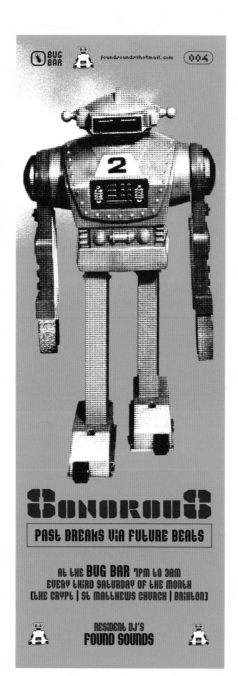

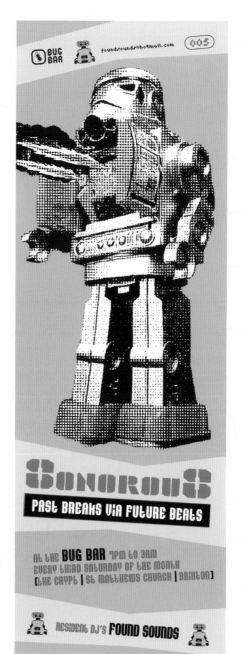

designed by: **Mitch**

designed by: **Mitch**

V5 LOU K. + BLAMI S6 MARKOS (castellòn) V12 M&M
S13 JORGE EXPLOSION (doctor EXPLOSION)
en acùstico,solitario y DJ + M&M V19 AMAYA
S20 CECILIA ANN + JEF LAG en Directo
presentacion libro benicassim. V26 BLAMI
S27 FROM HEAD TOTOE en Directo + M&M
V2 DE FEBRERO LA MALA RODRIGUEZ

Heineken

ZULO URTARRILA 2001

designed by: **Blami**

HOBBY PARTY
DISCOS
ANGELMOLINA

+ M&M

carhartt®

Zulo
2 - 2 - 02
24:00 - 10€
Anticipada en: - Zulo, Hobbi (Locenk...)
y Siplo 20 Info: SalaZulo @ YAHoo.com

designed by: **Blami**

EUSKOTREN LARUMBAT GAUEKO ZERBITZUA
DONOSTI-LASARTE : 23:19, 01:19, 03:19, 05:19
LASARTE-DONOSTI: 23:46, 01:46, 03:46, 05:46

ZULO AZAROA 2001
LASARTE

CONCIERTOS A LAS 23:00 DJ'S A LA 1

VIERNES: CHICO+BLAMI ✳ SÀBADO 3 : EL PAYO MALO (TARRASA-HIP-HOP) +
+ SYR (OLD SCHOOL)+KIGO+ EL NOTA ✳ VIERNES 9 POLAIN + LOU K (GADAFI)
SÀBADO 10: ARI (GERONA-HIP-HOP) + R DE RUMBA (DOBLE V-HIP-HOP FUNK+
BLAMI ✳ VIERNES 16 PATXI & TXARLY (BW) ✳ SÀBADO 17 FANGORIA-
(MADRID - POP) + NAIROBI TRÍO (BCN - VARIETES) ✳ VIERNES 23 MR SNOID+
SYR ✳ SÀBADO 24 M&M+ARAÑA VIERNES 30 BORJA (INTERMUSIC)
SÀBADO 1 DE DICIEMBRE SOLO LOS SOLO (GERONA-HIP-HOP) + M&M +
PEZ (ETXEKALTE) = ACID TRAXX PARTY ☼

✳ SI QUIERES RECIBIR NUESTRA PROGRAMACIÓN POR MENSAJES SMS
Y E-MAIL SOLO TIENES QUE DARNOS TUS DATOS. SALABULO@YAHOO.COM

Heineken **carhartt** OLD SCHOOL

Dubuffet+blami

designed by: **Blami**

ZULO

LASARTE MAYO 2001

CONCIERTOS A LAS ONCE EN PUNTO
V4 CULTURA PROBASE (POP ELECTR. JAEN) **S5 AVIADOR DRO** (TECH-POP MAD)
+MANUKIAN V11 FANG (ELECTROPOP BCN) **S26 STEREOSCOP** (POP MAD)

DISK-JOKEYS A LA UNA EN PUNTO
V4 ARAÑA S5 KOSMOS (COSMOSRECORDS BARCELONA) **+M&M V11 BLAMI**
S12 AMAYA CON LOU K V18 PATXI CON TXARLI S19 M&M
V25 DAVID DELOR (ANGLET) **+XAVIER** (X-LAB BURDEOS) **S26 M&M +KIGO**

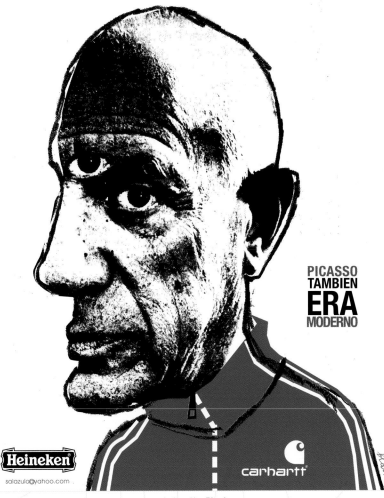

PICASSO
TAMBIEN
ERA
MODERNO

Heineken

salazulo@yahoo.com

carhartt

designed by: **Blami**

abril2001

zulo
lasarte

v6 dj alain (buena wista)
s7 niños mutantes (granada-pop)
+omar (bcn-minifunk-moog)) +m&m

x11 patxi & txarli (buena wista)
j12 syr + chip (castellòn)
v13 polain + lou k (hernani)
s14 m&m
v20 piramideaks (australia-power-pop)
+araña (donosti)
s21 ming (belgica-electro-pop)
+m&m + kigo
v27 blami
s28 an der beat (bcn-diskofuntech)
+ dj an der beat (minifunk)
+ m&m

Heineken
salazulo@yahoo.com

designed by: **Blami**

ZULO — SEPTIEMBRE 2001.

(DJ'S A LAS 24:00)

S1 SIDERAL (BCN) + M&M = 1000 PTS-
V7 BLAMJ (SIGLO 20).
S8 LOU K (GADAFI) + BLAMJ (SIGLO 20).
V14 ARAÑA (ETXEKALTE)-
S15 KIGO (ETXEKALTE) + M&M.
V21 PATXI & TXARLI (BUENA WISTA).
S22 M&M + ARAÑA (ETXEKALTE).
V28 DJ PLLX (DONOSTI).
S29 RUDE TAYLOR (BCN) + M&M = 1000 PTS.

* SI QUIERES RECIBIR NUESTRA PROGRAMACIÓN POR MENSAJES SMS
/ E-MAIL SOLO TIENES QUE DARNOS TUS DATOS.

designed by: **Blami**

La DINaMOFeBReRO2000.
DISCOTECNOHOUSEFUNKBREAKBEATDRUM&BASS segunda planta de itzela.
5. garcy noise (pamplona) + pi. 12. digitek festa 19. javi (pamplona) + xemark. 26. borja (intermusic) + blami.

(blami)

designed by: **Blami**

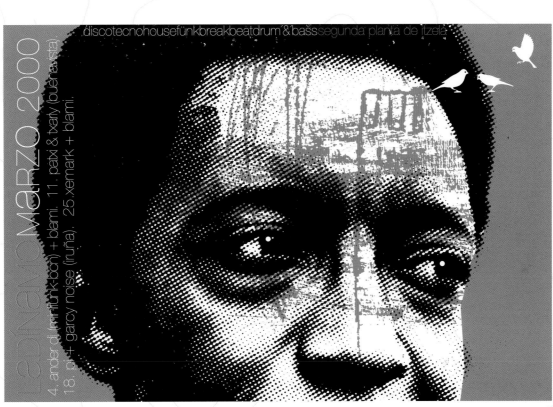

designed by: **Blami**

La dínamo

2ª PLANTA DE ITZELA. N- 1km. 470. A-8 Autopista. 3 Irtera. Oiartzun. Gipuzkoa.

AZAROA 1999

6. alain + blami. 13. alberto + alex. 20. blami + garay. 27. xemark + alberto.

IRAILA 1999

dinamo itzelako 2. solairuan dago.

11. garcy noise (iruña)+pi. 12. pi+blami. 25. xabl. v (konplot)+xemark.

ITZELA N- 1km 470 A-8 Autopista 3 Irten. Oiartzun. Donostia.

URRIA 1999

dinamo aretoa 24tik 7 arte irekita dago.

2. garcy noise + alberto. 9. pi + blami. 16. freakout+ xemark. 23. alberto + pi. 30. xemark + blami.

designed by: **Blami**

LADÍNAMO
APIRILA 2000
diskoteknohousefunkbreakbeatdrum'n'bass.
segunda planta de Itzela.

1. lou k (hernani) + blami. 8. juan carlos (bass reaction *france* kiko vinylo *spain*) + alex.
15. chico + garcy noise (Pamplona). 21. imanol (txill-aut txitxarro) + ladínamocrew.
22. javi (rayder eibar) + blami. 29. pedro destino + xemark.

designed by: **Blami**

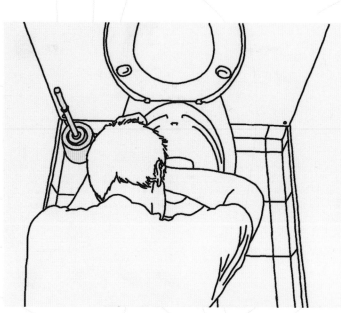

ITZELA. N-1Km. 470. A-8 Autopista. 3 Irtera. Oiartzun. Gipuzkoa.

URRIA 1999

larunbatero dinamo aretoa 24:00 H. tik aurrera.

2. garcy noise +xemark. 9. pi + blami. 11. ima (txill-aut txitxarro) contra blami .
16. freakout+alberto. 23. alberto + pi. 30. xemark + blami.

designed by: **Blami**

ITZELA N-1Km. 470,7 - A-8 Autopista 2 Irtera. Oiartzun. Donostia.

URRIA 1999

dinamo aretoa 24tik 7 arte irekita dago.

2. garcy noise + alberto. 9. pi + blami. 16. freackout + xemark. 23. alberto + pi. 30. xemark + blami.

designed by: **Blami**

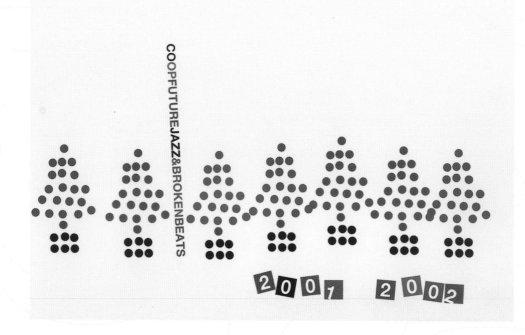

COOPFUTUREJAZZ&BROKENBEATS

2 0 0 1   2 0 0 2

APRIL **2002**   **COOP**
FUTUREJAZZ&BROKENBEATS

SUN MON TUE WED THU FRI SAT
8-1AM

FEB 10TH *PRE VALENTINES SPESH
1   2   ③   4   ⑤   6   **FEB 24TH / MAR 10TH**
                           MAR 31ST / APR 14TH / APR 28TH

7   8   9   10 11 12 13   **2ND & LAST SUNDAY EVERY MONTH**
                              SUNDAY / 7:30PM TILL 12AM / £5 ENTRY 4 ALL
                              THE VELVET ROOMS / 143 CHARING CROSS ROAD
⑭ ⑮ 16 17 18 19 ⑳   **LONDON W1**

21 22 23 24 25 26 27   RESIDENT DJ'S
                              I G CULTURE (NEW SECTOR MOVEMENTS)
                              DEGO (4HERO) **DEMUS** (NUMBERS)
㉘ 29 30
                              DJ'S ON ROTATION
                              PHIL ASHER / DOMU / SEIJI
                              AFRONAUGHT / ALEX ATTIAS
                              MODAJI / MIKE SLOCOMBE
                              BUGZ IN THE ATTIC / MARC MAC
                              info: coop@goyamusic.com
                              bookings: sahra@soniksuite.fsnet.co.uk

two thousand and two.
design: thanksandpraise

designed by: **Wadada**

designed by: **Wadada**

designed by: **Wadada**

designed by: **Wadada**

Blacktronica

IN DUB

Blacktronica

HOSTED BY CHARLIE DARK

designed by: **Wadada**

designed by: **Wadada**

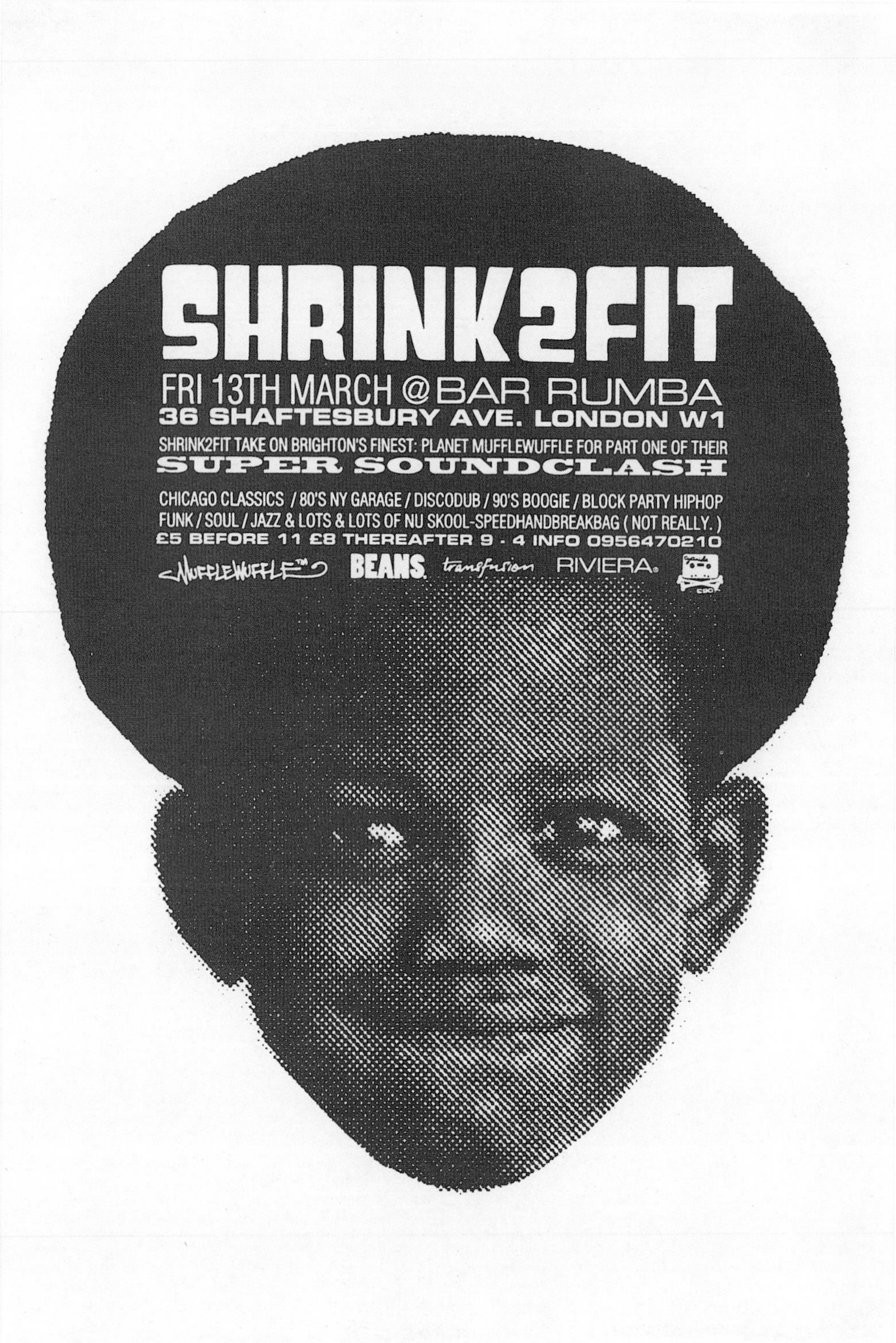

designed by: **Leo Elstob**

designed by: **Leo Elstob**

designed by: **Parra**

designed by: **Parra**

designed by: **Andrew Rae**

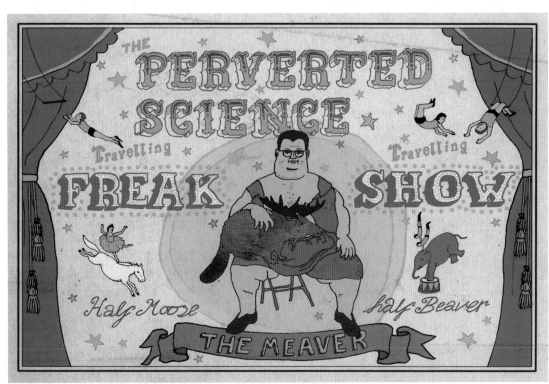

designed by: **Andrew Rae**

KINDRED SPIRITS IS SPONSORED BY STOLICHNAYA IS DESIGNED BY MACHINE www.ourmachine.com CAMEL

VAKZUID
Olympischstadion 35
Amsterdam
020 - 5708400
www.vakzuid.nl
info@vakzuid.nl

You can reach Vakzuid by nightbus nr 78, 71, 272 & 270
taxi Vakzuid - city centre 11,- euro

designed by: **Machine**

15.03.02

★ALMA HORTON

(4 HERO | KING BRITT)

MACHINE BEAMING

05.04.02

WONDERFULL★

STEVIE WONDER SPECIAL

BOBITTO
DJ SPINNA

VJ SUPREME CUISINE

19.04.02

BRAZIL SPECIAL | LIVE ON STAGE

AZYMUTH ★

PRESENTED BY
www.ourmachine.com

PARADISO

Alma Horton:
12 euro incl
open 23:00

Weteringschans 6
Amsterdam
020 - 6264521

designed by: **Machine**

KINDRED SPIRITS

IS DESIGNED BY MACHINE
www.oumachine.com

VAKZUID
Olympischstadion 35
Amsterdam
020 - 5708400
www.vakzuid.nl
info@vakzuid.nl

You can reach Vakzuid by nightbus nr 78, 71, 272 & 270 lines
taxi Vakzuid - city centre fl.25,-

designed by: **Machine**

KINDRED
SPIRITS

17.11.01
PARADISO
WETERINGSCHANS 6
SATURDAY Fl.35,-
OPEN 23:00

GUEST DJ'S DEGO (4 HERO) PHIL ASHER (RESTLESS SOUL)
LIVE ON STAGE MARK DE CLIVE-LOWE
WITH KAIDI THATHAM AND REEL PEOPLE

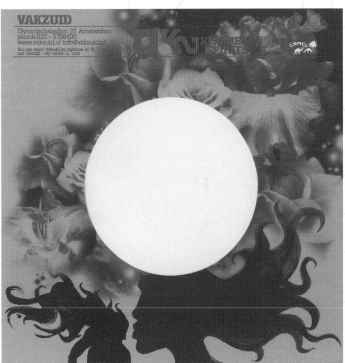

VAKZUID
Olympischstadion 35 Amsterdam
phone.020 - 5706400
www.vakzuid.nl info@vakzuid.nl
You can reach Vakzuid by nightbus nr 76, 77
last Vakzuid - city centre 11,- euro

KINDRED
SPIRITS

CAMEL

designed by: **Machine**

misc.

ARTWORKS BY: GARETH BAYLISS, BEN DRURY, SHIN,
SARTORIA, BLAMI, SHEPARD FAIREY, RAFFINERIE,
WADADA, HAL UDELL, LEO ELSTOB, VÅR, SWIFTY, AMY DAVIES.

designed by: **Gareth Bayliss**

designed by: **Ben Drury**

DADA

JUNIO
SÁBADO 16: FW BEATS * SÁBADO 23: LENCO "REVIVAL".
LUNES: KIGO "SAN PELAIO": KO'GIROA.
SÁBADO 30: BLAMI EXPONE Y PINTA CON CIEN FUEGOS.
EXPOSICIÓN IONE SAIZAR (FOTOGRAFÍA).

JULIO
SÁBADO 7: KIGO "SAN FERMÍN" * SÁBADO 14: CHICO.
SÁBADO 21: ARAÑA * MARTES 24: MARIO MAQUEDA.
SÁBADO 28: FW BEATS * LUNES: 30: MAKALA.
EXPOSICIÓN BLAMI (ARTISTA)

AGOSTO
SÁBADO 4: CHICO * SÁBADO 11: MAKALA.
MIÉRCOLES 15: KIGO * SÁBADO 18: ARAÑA.
SÁBADO 25: MARIO MAQUEDA.
EXPOSICIÓN JOSE CHABALÍN (ARTISTA)

SEPTIEMBRE
SÁBADO 1: FW BEATS * SÁBADO 8: LENCO.
DOMINGO 9: KIGO "FIESTA VASCA" * SÁBADO 15: CHICO.
EXPOSICIÓN ZUHAR (FOTOGRAFÍA).

NUESTRA SOLIDARIDAD CON EL ZULO DE LASARTE.
NO AL DESPOTISMO.

uda
dada
summer
ètè 2001
estate
Zarautz

carhartt

blami*

designed by: **Blami**

designed by: **Shepard Fairey**

SA. 25.05.2002
STRAIGHTAHEADREC.& WAGGON/B13 PRESENTS:

SPREAD LOVE

DJ VOLCOV (MILANO /RIMA/ARCHIVE)
DJ ALEX DALLAS (ZH//STRAIGHT AHEAD REC.)

DOORS.23.00 UHR
BOGEN13
VIADUKTSTR.13 3005 ZH

designed by: **Raffinerie**

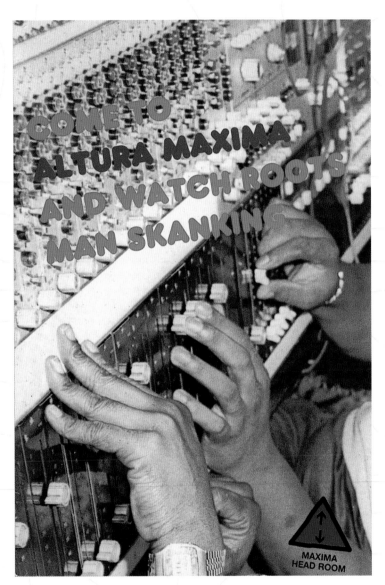

designed by: **Wadada**

DUSTED.

2

バウンティ・ハンタ

THE
BOUNTY
HUNTER
SESSIONS

バウンティ・ハンタ

DUSTED. 2

designed by: **Ben Drury**

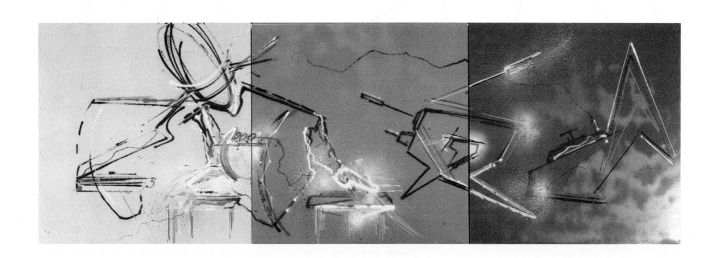

FABRICLIVE

UNKLESOUNDS

designed by: **Ben Drury** - artwork by: **Futura**

designed by: **Hal Udell**

Shrink2Fit New Years Eve 96 **97**

Shrink2Fit New Years Eve 96 **97**
9pm till 5am At the Regent Film Studios, St. Leonards Rd. London NW10 (Nearest tube North Acton)
This Party is strictly for invite holders only / Info 0956 470210

434

434

designed by: **Leo Elstob**

*author unknown

author unknown

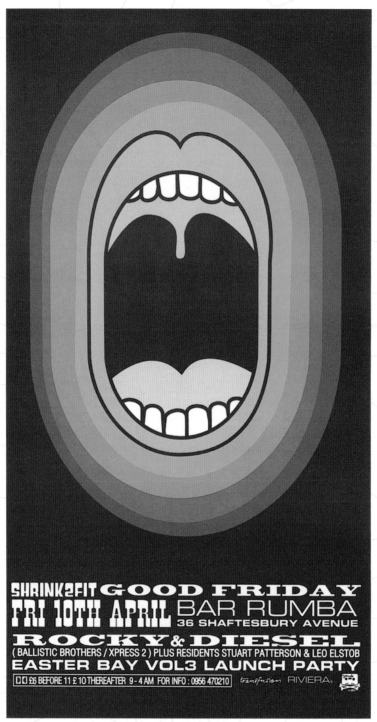

designed by: **Leo Elstob**

designed by: **Vår**

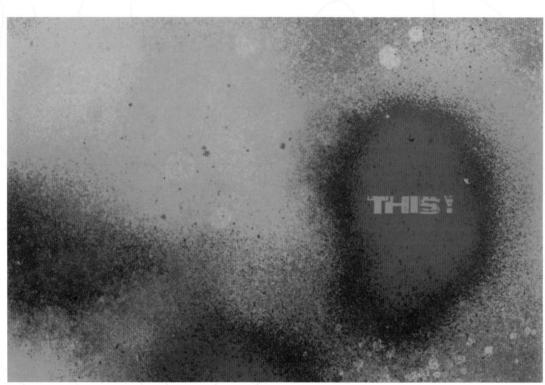

designed by: **Swifty**

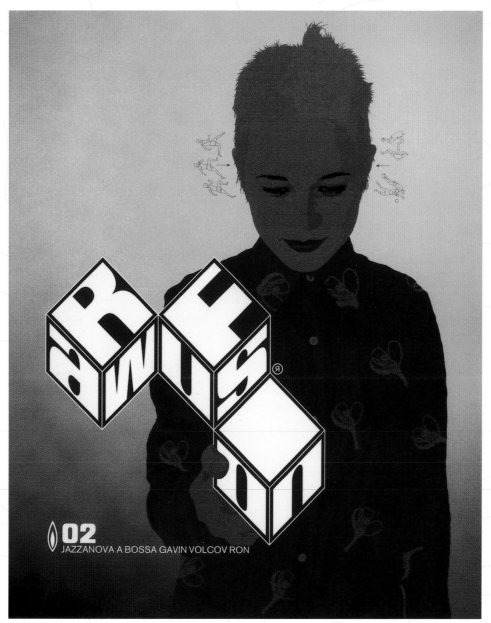

designed by: **Vâr**

designed by: **Amy Davies**

BOXING DAY PARTY THE SURGERY

A NIGHT OF 100% SOUL. TWO FLOORS OF PURE SOULFUL GROOVES. MAIN ROOM: THE SURGERY, A SELECTION OF 70'S AND 80'S NU SOUL GROOVES. GROUND FLOOR: 60'S, 70'S AND MODERN SOUL. THE NIGHT WILL FEATURE DJ'S BOB JONES, CJ, STEVE HOBBS AND THE JONES BOYS (TERRY AND IVOR) THURSDAY 26TH DECEMBER, 10PM-3AM £8/£6 CONCS. AT THE BLUE NOTE, 1 HOXTON SQUARE, LONDON, N1. T: 0171 729 8440. PARKING LIMITED. THE BLUE NOTE CLUB CULTURE AVAILABLE ON CD, MC, DOUBLE LP AND LIMITED EDITION BLUE VINYL.

DESIGN: AMY DAVIES & DANIELLE CAMPBELL

designed by: **Amy Davies**

designed by: **Shin**

designed by: **Sartoria** - artwork by: **Giulia Benini**

straight ahead presents:
forward

SONNTAG
22.10.
free entry
opening night:
djs:
alex dallas (earthbound)
& roberto ceschi (sequel)

SONNTAG
29.10.
free entry
djs:
simone serritella (big bang ,
solaria/far out rec., london)
& gianni siravo (sequel)

every sunday, 9pm at club zodiac, spitalgasse 5, zürich dance
session for open-minded & forward thinkin people, be there early!

designed by: **Raffinerie**

designed by: **Raffinerie**

designed by: **Swifty**

24/10/02

Hi MATTEO.

HERE'S SOME
FLYERS FOR YA!

ENJOY!

NO NEED TO RETURN
THEM - YOU CAN KEEP
THEM!

BEN.

MAT,
SOME MORE FLYERS
I FOUND,
THE .BRAZILIAN LOVE
AFFAIR FIT TOGETHER
LIKE SO.!

Swifty

YO MAT -
REQUESTED FLYERS
ENCLOSED.
LOOKING FORWARD
TO SEEING THE
BOOK.

LATER DAWG!

MITCH.

Hey Matt.!
Here You Go all the flyers.
You wanted and did not want
let me know when You finish the
book.!

Succes.

Parra

Amsterdam
23 - 9 - 2002

Hi Mat
hope you enjoy
them as much
as I have designing
them. you should do
an exhibition. peace Robi

JAZZ SECTION

BRASILIAN SECTION

HIP HOP SECTION

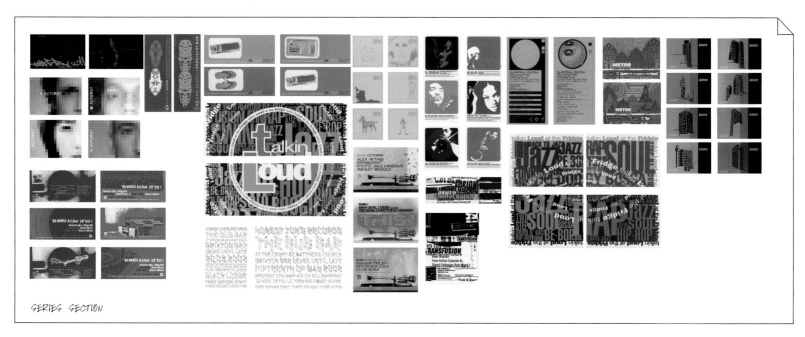

SERIES SECTION

DRAWING SECTION

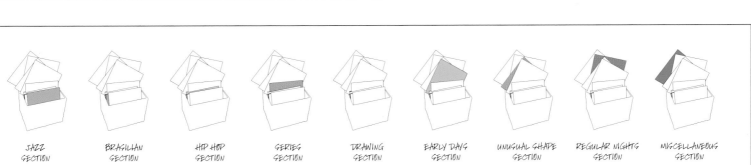

JAZZ
SECTION

BRASILIAN
SECTION

HIP HOP
SECTION

SERIES
SECTION

DRAWING
SECTION

EARLY DAYS
SECTION

UNUSUAL SHAPE
SECTION

REGULAR NIGHTS
SECTION

MISCELLANEOUS
SECTION

THIS BOOK IS
AN INSANE
IDEA OF:

*THE DESIGNERS INVOLVED:

ADRIAN SELF and MAT DANGERMOUSE
ALI AUGUR
ANDREW ARNOLD
ANDY RAE
ANDY WARD
AUTOMAT
AZLAN DESIGN
BEN DRURY
BEN SWIFT
BLAM!
DAVE KINSEY
DANILO BETTONI
FORM03
GARETH BAYLISS
GRAHAM BATES
HAL UDELL
HEAVYWEIGHT PROD.
LEO ELSTOB
MACHINE
MITCH
MODE2
PARRA
PAUL ALLEN
RAFFINERIE
RAPHAEL BARTELS
SARTORIA
SHARP
SHEPARD FAIREY
SWIFTY
TYLER ASKEW
TOM HINGSTON
VÅR
WADADA

THANKS SO MUCH FOR YOUR KINDNESS + JOINTWORK.
-> THIS BOOK WOULDN'T HAVE BEEN POSSIBLE WITHOUT YOU.

GRAZIE!

ADRIAN SELF + MAT DANGERMOUSE
(C/O SOUNDS OF THE UNIVERSE)
7 BROADWICK STREET
LONDON W1F 0DA
U.K.

AUTOMAT

AUTOMAT
JÜRGEN BAUER AND LLEWELLEN HEILI
RAMPERSTORFFERGASSE 41/6
1050 VIENNA
AUSTRIA

TEL +43.1.712 22 61
FAX +43.1.718 19 80

WWW.AUTOMAT.AT
PRO@AUTOMAT.AT

GARETH BAYLISS

GEBAYLISS@HOTMAIL.COM

ALI AUGUR
ALIAUGUR@MAC.COM
WWW.ALIAUGUR.COM

TEL +44.7976 245 010

AZLAN DESIGN
BRISTOL
U.K.

WWW.AZLANDESIGN.COM

GRAHAM BATES
322C HACKNEY ROAD
LONDON
E2 7AX
U.K.

TEL +44 (0) 781 848 6450

INFO@GRAHAMBATES.COM
WWW.GRAHAMBATES.COM

aagd

ANDREW ARNOLD
"AA GRAPHIC DESIGN"
HAAGER STRASSE 10
D-81671 MÜNCHEN
GERMANY

TEL +49.89.610 69 16
FAX +49.89.610 11 834

HQ@AAGD.DE
WWW.AAGD.DE

BEN SWIFT/ NONSINTHETIK
120 HORN LANE
ACTON
LONDON
W3 6NY
U.K.

TEL +44 (0)7939 221 359

WWW.NONSINTHETIK.COM (COMING SOON!)
NONSINTHETIK@HOTMAIL.COM

HAL UDELL

HALLAM@MAC.COM

ANDREW RAE
9 DOWNSIDE LODGE
29 UPPER PARK RD
LONDON
NW3 2UY
U.K.

+44(0)20 7449 9136
+44(0)116 500 8636
A@ANDREWRAE.ORG.UK
WWW.ANDREWRAE.ORG.UK

BLAMI.

JOSE ANTONIO IGLESIAS MORENO
LOREAK MENDIAN (BLAMI)
AVENIDA LETXUNBORRO 57
IRUN 20305
SAN SEBASTIAN (GUIPUZCOA)
ESPAÑA

TEL +34 943 667271
FAX +34 943 610277

BLAMI@LOREAKMENDIAN.COM

heavyweight

HEAVYWEIGHT PRODUCTION HOUSE
24 AVENUE MONT ROYAL. 0. #704A
MONTRÉAL, QC. CANADA
H2T 2S2
U.S.A.

TEL. 514 840 7215
FAX. 514 288 0535

WWW.HVW8.COM

ANDY WARD
79 TAVISTOCK CRESCENT
LONDON
W11 1AD
U.K.

WWW.ANDYWARD.CO.UK
ANDY@ANDYWARD.CO.UK

DANILO BETTONI A.K.A. REO FROM TDK
C/O GLAM JAM
VIA LUIGI TURCHI, 1/3
44100 FERRARA
ITALY

DANILO@GLAMJAM.IT

DAVE KINSEY

INFO@KINSEYVISUAL.COM
WWW.KINSEYVISUAL.COM

WWW.BLKMRKT.COM

 **FORM03**
AGENTUR FÜR GRAFIKDESIGN UND FOTOGRAFIE

FORM03
BODENSEESTRAßE 51
D-88048 FRIEDRICHSHAFEN

TEL + 49 75 41 59 95 21
FAX + 49 75 41 59 95 28

KONTAKT@FORM03.DE

PARRA
DE WITTENSTRAAT 25
1052 AK AMSTERDAM
N.L.

TEL. +31 6 289 55509

PARRA@BLAMMO.NL

TOM HINGSTON STUDIO LTD
16 BREWER STREET
LONDON W1F 9TX
ENGLAND

F. 0201 281 6048

INFO@HINGSTON.NET

---

leo elstob

LEO ELSTOB
LITTLE BRAZIERS FARM
BELLINGDON
CHESHAM
BUCKS
HP5 2UN
U.K.

TEL +44 (0) 1951 221 168

LEO.ELSTOB@BTINTERNET.COM

 **Raffinerie**

RAFFINERIE
AG FÜR GESTALTUNG
ANWANDSTRASSE 62
8004 ZÜRICH
CH

TEL. +43 322 11 11
FAX. +43 322 11 10

TYLER ASKEW
271 CLERMONT AVE.
NO. 3
BROOKLYN, NY 11205
U.S.A.

TEL. 917 602 8483

WWW.TYLERASKEW.COM
INFO@TYLERASKEW.COM

MACHINE

MACHINE
(MARK KLAVERSTIJN + PAUL DU BOIS-REYMOND)
DE WITTENSTR 25 1052 AK
AMSTERDAM
NL

TEL. +31 20 6862538

WWW.OURMACHINE.COM
WE@OURMACHINE.COM

SHEPARD FAIREY
LOS ANGELES, CA
U.S.A.

WWW.OBEYGIANT.COM
WWW.BLKMRKT.COM
AMANDA@OBEYGIANT.COM

VÅR
ROSLAGSGATAN 21 / GÅNGEN
SE-113 55 STOCKHOLM
S

TEL. +46 8 612 06 00

BJORN@WOO.SE

MITCH A.K.A. MITCHYBWOY

MITCHY.BWOY@VIRGIN.NET

SARTORIA

INFO@SARTORIA.COM

WADADA / THANKSANDPRAISE
31 BIRCH HOUSE
DROOP STREET
LONDON
W10 4EQ
U.K.

LEANNE@THANKSANDPRAISE.CO.UK

MODE 2

UK TEL. +44 1960 585 261
FR TEL. +33 6 10 78 66 09

MODE2@MODE2.ORG

SWIFTY

FAX. +44 0208 991 6812

WWW.SWIFTY.CO.UK
SWIFTY@SWIFTY.CO.UK

⌘loqobar

RAPHAEL BARTELS

RAPHAEL.BARTELS@RESULTDDB.NL

01.MODE 02.ANDY WARD 03.SHEPARD FAIREY 04.RAPHAEL BARTELS 05.DANILO BETTONI 06.MACHINE 07.CARLO "DON CORLEONE" GOLA 08.PARRA 09.MARCO GOLA 10.TYLER ASKEW 11.MY FAMILY STAND
12.SIMONE + MAT 13.LUCA BENINI 14.FRASER COOKE 15.ROBI + LEANNE 16.GENE STARSHIP (LEFT) + TYLER GIBNEY (CENTER) + DAN BULLER (RIGHT)=HEAVYWEIGHT 17.SEISHO SUMIDA 18.ENRICO 19.DAVE KINGSEY
20.RITA 21.PHIL REES 22. RAFFINERIE 23.SIMONE SERRITELLA 24.BEN SWIFT 25.GIOVANNI DE MARCHI 26.ANDY RAE 27.GARETH BAYLISS 28.CARLO + RITA al GALLO D'ORO 29.BLAM! 30.ALI AUGUR
31.LEO ELSTOB 32. ANDREW ARNOLD 33.FABIO CAPETTI 34.HAL UTELI 35.MATCH 36.GRAHAM BATES 37.CHMTD 38.ENRICO + MATTEO 39.IAN SWIFT 40.MARCO + MATTEO 41.ANTONIO 42.VED

MY INFINITE GRATITUDE GOES TO ->

MY FAMILY !

CARLO
RITA
MARCO

I WILL BE ETERNALLY GRATEFUL TO THE
FOLLOWING PERSONS FOR THE SUPPORT
THEY DECIDED TO GIVE TO THIS BOOK.

FABIO "SAMPRAS" CALEFFI
MARC "PATROL" FRASER
SIMONE "NOT ALWAYS ARGIONABLE" SERRITELLA
ENRICO "KUBRICK" CRIVELLARO
NINNI "STAY FREE" DE MARCHI
LUCA "BAIA" BENINI

THE "U.S.A." FAMILY:
KING BRITT
JEFF STAPLE
AMANDA at "BLKMRKT" L.A.
ANDREW JARVIS + ANDREW ENOCH

THE "AMSTERDAM" FAMILY:
DELTA
CHRISTIAAN at RUSH HOUR
STEVEN DE PEVEN
MOCKY

THE "LONDON" FAMILY:
MICHAEL KOPELMAN
ADE at PLASTIC PEOPLE
WILLIAM DOWLER
ALEX ATTIAS
LUCIA POSSAS
STUART + ANGELA at THE SOUND OF UNIVERSE
YURI + LAURENT at BOND INTERNATIONAL
PETE HERBERT

THE "BOLOGNA" FAMILY:
ANDY HOLISTER
PAOLO "CHELLI" + MATTEO "GABU" at RENOGRAFICA
MASSIMO + DARIO at SYNTHETICA
ANTONIO + GIUSALBERTO at A.G.O.

THE "JAPAN" FAMILY:
MEGU
YUKI
GEISHO

THE "ZURICH" FAMILY:
ROBERT MAYER + RITA
ALEX DALLAS

THE "STOCHOLM" FAMILY:
JASPER at DISCO STHLM

proud2beaflyer.com

mat-design.com

happybooks.it

slamjam.it

arision.net

neroli.it

foot-patrol.com

Printed in Italy
by renografica Bologna
May 2003

second release
September 2004